Crisis

CRISIS

Psychological First Aid for Recovery and Growth

by Ann S. Kliman

With a Foreword by ALBERT J. SOLNIT, M.D.

Jason Aronson Inc.

Northvale, New Jersey
London

The dialogue in this book is accurate to the best of my recollection and extensive notes. Some of the patients I depict represent composites, others are based on individuals; no one exclusively represents any real person, yet I hope that every one represents a part of each of us.

To Sam

CONTENTS

Foreword

The theoretical background of Ann S. Kliman's book extends back to the discoveries of Sigmund Freud and, more recently, from the models of Anna Freud's and Dorothy Burlingham's intervention and studies of deprived children in Vienna, of children at risk in blitz-torn London, of blind children, and of children threatened by handicap and loss. The construct that guides the author's initial approach is the psychoanalytic theory of trauma. With this theory, behavioral scientists have discovered that each person has a tolerance for what he or she can bear before being overwhelmed temporarily or permanently by massive loss or insult, or by the cumulative impact of repeated trauma. Developmental capabilities also set a limit on what can be tolerated. Other crucial factors are those of endowment, experience, and the social cushioning, or lack of it, that each person's community, culture, and ideological beliefs can offer. In addition to using trauma theory imaginatively, Ann Kliman has refined and elaborated its utilization. Beyond her scientific ken, she has tapped our oldest source of knowledge and wisdom, that which precedes and must overbalance nature's cruelty and man's inhumanity to man. The human child is helpless at birth and, through a long period of development, requires the protection, stimulation, and continuity of care by loving adults that can provide him with survival and a life worth living. Sudden trauma exposes each of its victims to such needs.

In writing this book, Ann Kliman has provided us with knowledge for the head and nurture for the heart. She has affectively reached out to those who have been struck by fate or by interpersonal tragedies in a manner that deprives them of the explanations they might seek in religion, philosophy, or ideology. She has been especially cognizant of children, for Ann Kliman is a Child Advocate who understands the child's need for affection, protection, and guidance by those adults—the parents—who make a permanent commitment to their children.

Throughout the book, the author's grasp of family autonomy as a fundamental condition to respect and to strengthen is expressed most eloquently. She understands that the child can be helped most effectively when parents voluntarily seek assistance for their children and themselves. She describes the theory of therapeutic intervention and its applications in recognizing, communicating about, and coping with the loss and trauma of death, injury, biological deficit, illness, divorce, rape, incest, and suicide.

With theoretical and clinical know-how, Ann Kliman demonstrates the most sophisticated understanding of how supportive alliances can be established, how to enable children and their parents to be active on their own behalf, and how to accept the limitations of our pain and knowledge. The sophistication is jargon-free and filled with the warmth of this Child Advocate's humanity and sensitivity.

The author veers away from the temptation to simplify what cannot be simple. She describes the suffering and realistically points out the painful work and long time involved if tragic challenge is to be transformed into psychological and emotional relief and mastery. Children and their parents are supported as they accept what cannot be changed, mobilize their personal and family resources, and, with Ann Kliman's sensitivity, skill, and emotional "loan," help themselves to move on to the life that remains and the future that is available.

She teaches from case histories, each of which is a mosaic made up of parts of many clinical experiences in providing first aid for situational crises. This method protects privacy and confidentiality while maximizing the usefulness of "selected" case illustrations.

I should warn the readers that this book serves a contrast between the hardheaded recognition and conviction that each of us must take responsibility for our reactions in coping with tragedy, and the openhearted engagement of a therapist who offers more than first aid. This contrast will bring tears to many readers' eyes because the themes are universal and the author knows how to reach her readers as well as her patients. She opens doors, provides choices that hadn't seemed to exist, and shows a blend of precise knowledge, sensitive use of self, and warm humanity to those with whom she is in touch. Ann Kliman is realistic, but she is also a tinge on the side of optimism, reflecting her therapeutic capability and outlook.

Like the poet Alfred Noyes, she brings us a universal view:

And all around the organ there's a sea without a shore
Of human joys and wonders and regrets
To remember and to recompense the music evermore
For what the cold machinery forgets.

Albert J. Solnit, M.D.

Acknowledgments

To all the people who have allowed me to enter their lives and helped me to help them; to the staff of the Center for Preventive Psychiatry, who have been a willing support system as well as a source of expertise; to Jodie Kliman, Ph.D., who shared her experience in family and network intervention and gave skillful encouragement; to David Kliman, who refreshed me with humor and provocative questions; to Steven Kliman, who actively and determinedly steered me toward community education; and to Eileen Goldfeder, M.S.W., who made this new edition a reality.

Crisis

We Are All Victims

If we could plan our lives to follow a certain ideal course—could fashion our destinies according to whatever principles of fulfillment, pleasure, and gain we hold most valid and appealing—we probably wouldn't think of programming into such a future any of even the most expectable crises of life. No one would have to suffer a crippling accident, be born with a severe handicap, or undergo hospitalization for an extended period; none of us would have to suffer a wrenching separation, would ever be violently assaulted, or have to die prematurely. In a word, we would never be victimized, whether by others or by fate.

We know, of course, that such guarantees are impossible, and we even, to a small degree, will anticipate some of these unwanted things happening to us, and without being considered overly gloomy or pessimistic. It is expected that we take out life insurance, draw up wills, cover ourselves and our families with financial protection against hospitalizing illness or accidental injury; and we are encouraged to educate ourselves to physical first aid.

But what of nonfinancial, nonphysical insurance? How are we expected to cope with the emotional and psychological effects of sudden crises?

Expression of anguish and grief and reaction to victimization have been among the strongest and most pervasive undercurrents of human history. They have provided the thematic substance of legend, myth, fiction, poetry, and drama of cultures East and West. They have been painted on cave walls, gourds, paper, and canvas. They have been beaten out by a single player on a handmade drum and played by a full orchestra in a crowded concert hall. They have been expressed by an individual shivering in isolation, and by an entire community united in ritual dance. But only since the 1940s has any systematic attempt been made to understand the psychology of victimization.

World War II taught us more than we wished to know about victimization . . . when we went into the concentration camps, when we dared to face the survivors of Hiroshima and Nagasaki. But we did learn, and the lesson was important: when a disaster or tragedy strikes, no one escapes.

In the professional terms of clinical psychology, victims fall into three broad categories. People who are killed or injured are the *direct victims*. The family, friends, and neighbors of the killed or injured, and those who live through the tragedy and emerge physically unhurt, are the *indirect victims*. The largest group of all are the *hidden victims*, the care-givers—doctors, nurses, social workers, psychologists, clergy, police, fire fighters, agency and school personnel; those of us who by training and experience deliver human service.

The dangers inherent in all three types of victimization have become quite clear. Those direct victims who have physically survived tend to suffer from anxiety, depression, feelings of helplessness, inadequacy, fears of repetition of the trauma, loss of appetite, and sleep problems. Indirect victims tend to suffer primarily from guilt reactions now commonly known as "guilt of the survivor." Such guilt is symptomatically expressed most frequently in the onset of new physical and psychosomatic illness, in increased family disputes, and in a rise in the accident rate—at home, on the road, at school, and at work. We professionals in the third group, we hidden victims, suffer from a special disadvantage. We're rarely aware we are being victimized. After all, we're highly trained and vastly experienced; we're just doing our job. But in our attempt to do that job, we often fall into the trap of *doing for* the victims we are trying to help. Rather than facilitate the victims *to do for themselves*, we succumb to omnipotent rescue fantasies and perceive the victims as too helpless, sick, or frightened to make decisions or care for themselves. Ironically, such ministrations serve only to revictimize victims; to keep them in a passive, dependent position, often infantilized. No wonder such victims do not heal quickly, are unable to reassume responsibilities or to adapt to their pain. Then what happens to the care-givers? We can't blame the victim for our feeling tired, irritable, frustrated, and unsuccessful, so we deny or avoid such uncharitable, "unprofessional" feelings. Yet despite our best efforts not to let our feelings show, they leak out. At these times we are apt to get into arguments with our co-workers, pick fights with our spouses, yell at the kids, and resort to tranquilizers. And we still feel rotten.

The special demands and problems of hidden victims are most apparent in the communal aftermaths of natural and mass disasters such as floods, tornadoes, earthquakes, plane crashes, and widespread fires, and although I have directed two psychological first-aid programs following such disasters—one after Hurricane Agnes in Corning, New York, in 1972, and the other following a tornado in Xenia, Ohio, in 1974—our concern in this book is family situations. Still, insofar as the indirect victims of family situations find themselves in care-giver roles, the symptoms experienced by the professional hidden victims will often be manifested in their cares too, as well as in the self-regard of direct victims.

It is human nature to rally around when there is need. Most of us will give the proverbial shirt off our backs to the destitute, and will listen with sympathy and understanding to the expressions of fear and pain, even the demandingness of direct victims—as long as their complaints don't last too long, and as long as we feel our efforts and commiserations are appreciated. But then a certain ethic intervenes. We live in a society that believes in "pulling oneself up by one's bootstraps"; a culture that expects us to "keep a stiff upper lip," "act like a man," and "get on with the job." We can accept the time and work it takes for a burn to heal or a bone to set, but we have less tolerance and understanding for the time it takes for psychological injuries to heal. And just as we can become intolerant of others who are direct victims, we can turn intolerant, critical, and judgmental of ourselves. We are embarrassed and ashamed when we cry "for no reason," when we feel jittery, can't sleep, have nightmares, or just don't feel and act as we used to. We begin to think we are "going crazy," that we are weak and incompetent. We become afraid to share our anxieties lest they be confirmed by others, and the more others treat us with kid gloves or get angry because we aren't behaving as they think we should, the more isolated we feel, and the less able to cope efficiently we become. Besides, isn't it stronger, kinder, and more caring to protect those we love from such distress? Doesn't it make it worse to dwell on it? "If I let my child see me cry she'll think that I'm weak and that will only scare her more." "My husband has so many things to worry about, I can't burden him with my feelings." "My mother is so old and frail, it would kill her to know that Joe has leukemia."

We are selective about the feelings we are able to share with others—comfortable if sharing happiness, humor, or compassion, if we are demonstrating our courage, dignity, unselfishness, or determination; hesitant when we feel frightened, angry, needy, or tearful. We feel ashamed and belittled at these times, and don't want others to know it, as if such human reactions to severe stress should be alien to us, or on the assumption that the only allowable part of being human is the noble part.

Perhaps the most important point this book has to make is that people victimized by an acute situational crisis are *entitled* to feel whatever they feel. Responses to loss, illness, abuse, or displacement are usually neither neurotic nor psychotic; they are an *adjustment reaction* to the acute stress. Such diagnosis implies no pathology; it does imply a heightened vulnerability, a danger point. If the danger is acknowledged, we then have an opportunity to explore it and seek out the most adaptive, least destructive ways of living through it and mastering it.

An acute situational crisis activates psychological defenses that help us bear whatever misfortune has befallen us. They are the mind's protective device, nature's way of allowing us to continue functioning. But such defenses are usually unconscious; we are not aware of them, nor do we control them. We do not deliberately decide: "My boss is such a tyrant and makes me feel so demeaned, I'll just start making things tough for my subordinates so I can feel good and strong again" *(identification with the aggressor)*; or "I'm much too terrified to find out why the sore on my lip won't heal, so I'll just ignore it and it'll probably go away" *(avoidance, denial)*; or "It's too scary and sad to cry about Grandpa's death, so when the cookies are gone I'll cry about that" *(displacement)*.

Protective as they are, defenses are as likely to be *maladaptive* as *adaptive*. One defense frequently activated by an acute crisis is *regression*, the return to an earlier stage of development, particularly that phase of childhood known as *magical thinking*. Essentially, magical thinking is the belief that anything we think, wish, fear, dream, or say *makes things happen*. It is a normal developmental phase of all children under age eight. To give one example: I knew a bright and healthy five-year-old who, following an argument with his mother, went outside, picked up his brother's baseball bat, and with all of his little-boy fury banged it against a light pole. At that instant all the lights in his home went out, all the lights on the block went out. When his parents finally found where he was hiding, he cried, "I didn't mean to break all the lights, I didn't!" What he couldn't know was that in the instant he had hit the pole, all the lights on the East Coast had gone out. It was the blackout of 1965! He could imagine only that his anger had been strong and powerful enough to have stopped all the electricity in his neighborhood.

Magical thinking is not only indulged in by children, it is an adjustment reaction for most severely stressed adults. How often have you heard someone impose guilt on himself, say, following an auto accident: "If only I hadn't sent her on that errand!"; or, following an infant's fall: "If only I hadn't been taking a shower!" If only, if only—as if we had the omnipotence to control life and death, or the omniscience to read the future. So common are such reactions that we have given them a label: "the if-only syndrome." The syndrome is manifested not only in the regressive pull of the stressed adult, but in all the pervasive guilt that assails the families of direct victims.

Since magical thinking is so typical of reactions in situational crises, and because children are so often caught in the middle of family traumas, let's look briefly at some traditional attitudes toward childhood. In the Middle Ages, children were viewed as mere homunculi, miniature adults with all the attributes, abilities, and disabilities of their parents. The attitude of the Victorian era was hardly more sympathetic—children were seen as unformed, uncivilized wee animals who were acceptable only as long as they didn't interrupt the adult world, as long as they were "seen but not heard." Sometime during this century, perhaps in overcompensation for such demeaning attitudes, children became perceived primarily in terms of their developmental vulnerability, as little ones who needed to be protected from the nastiness and excitement of the adult world. Children became—in my husband's phrase—our "islands of innocence." Whenever we act as if children do not know and cannot understand, we ourselves, for that moment, do not know and understand. And in this act of caring, we impose a difficult and sometimes overwhelming burden on children. Even very young children are aware of and sensitive to significant changes in the attitudes, behavior, and tones of those around them. When we do not acknowledge why Mom is crying on the phone, or Dad is so cranky, or Grandma doesn't want to play, or Johnny isn't there, young children, sensing how different everyone is acting, believe it's their fault. It is hard enough for a child to learn to distinguish between dream and actuality, between wish and enactment, between pretend and real, without having adults add to the confusion. For children, the grimmest reality is rarely as terrifying as their own fantasy.

Of course children play into our misguided evaluations of their strengths and vulnerabilities because they *are* developmentally immature. Children have short attention spans. They may cry bitterly one moment and then appear happy and involved the next. They seem not to care about sad events for very long, and they seem to forget easily. (And since we often wish that they could forget, we comfort ourselves with the thought that they do.)

If we tell a child that someone they loved has died, they may cry for a few seconds or not at all, and then demand an ice cream cone or run to watch television. We interpret such behavior as proof children "don't care" and "don't understand." In truth, the child is expressing as much feeling as he *dares,* then running off to recuperate. This is precisely when we need to make ourselves available to our children, at their level, at their pace.

Admittedly, such sensitivity to even our own beloved child is difficult when we too are bereft and hurting. But as we give sustenance to our children in time of crisis, so can they give sustenance to us. Kids are likely to "say it like it is," and what they say is often what we're feeling but are afraid to express. Our ability to nurture children at times of extreme stress can serve to reassure us of our ability to manage our lives, which in turn lessens our own sense of helplessness and passivity.

In an attempt to protect our children (and ourselves) from pain, discomfort, and confusion, we deprive them of the opportunity to ingest small, tolerable doses of sadness and anxiety, doses which could strengthen them for possibly larger, more unexpected and uncontrollable assaults to come. When we allow ourselves to be medically inoculated, we expose our bodies to a small dose of a disease-causing germ. The dose is large enough to put the body's immunologic defenses to work, but small enough not to overwhelm or destroy those defenses. We see evidence that the immunization is working when a small tender or itchy area appears, or when we feel slightly sick after the shot. Because children do not have sufficient maturity to pay constant attention to anything for very long, and because children can be overwhelmed by their own thoughts and fantasies, they tend to protect themselves by accepting disturbing perceptions bit by bit. A girl who appears to be playing unconcernedly in the sandbox several days after her grandmother has died and is repeatedly covering a doll with sand may well be using the familiar play as a way of expressing her thoughts and feelings about her grandmother's death and burial—events in which the child may not have participated, but about which she has overheard and observed a great deal. This dosing of bearable bits of painful or sad feelings through the vehicle of play can teach us much about the world of the child—and of the adult.

Victimization by pseudoprotection is the fate not only of children, but of all people whom we, as responsible adults, see as vulnerable and needy. Especially disadvantaged by overprotective family and cultural attitudes are the elderly. Because Grandpa had a heart attack last year, we really do not want to upset him by telling him that Pete broke his shoulder playing football. When we go to visit him next week, we'll say that Pete had to study for an exam, or had to be at football practice, or had a bad cold. And if Junior lets something slip, well, Grandpa is a little hard of hearing and we can just tell him that he misunderstood. And certainly Grandma, who is having so much trouble with her back, shouldn't be told that Sissie dropped out of school and is living in the city. Grandma just wouldn't understand such things, she would be so worried, and we don't want to upset her at her age.

Again we are infantilizing, even abusing, those closest to us, in this case our own elderly. We rationalize it as for their own good, but by denying them their rightful functioning within the family network we are revictimizing them. And we place an additional burden on ourselves. We must play out a charade of pretense, and few of us can carry this off. The pressure of pretending steals energy desperately needed for coping, sharing, and problem solving—energy already drained by the crisis. When we infantilize the adults of our families—our parents, spouses, and grandparents—we forget they have been functioning for forty, fifty, sixty years, and are long familiar with disappointments and grief, probably through many more traumatic events than we have known. What may not be familiar to them is the sense of being thought helpless or useless, and sadly, inevitably, the more we treat people as unable to cope, the less able they are to cope. And to help us.

In this age of plastic products, pocket computers, and supersonic transportation, human values and interactions need ever more tender nurturing and conservation. We can commit ourselves to saving an endangered species of wildlife, or preserving a tract of wilderness, but how unecological of us to waste our nearest and most precious natural resource—our own families.

Often when I teach or lecture I'm asked how I can be so determinedly sure about what I say. It's a fair question. My professional experience is primarily with the Center for Preventive Psychiatry, a nonprofit community agency in White Plains, New York, founded in 1965. Preventive psychiatry is relatively new in both medicine and psychology. The Center's uniqueness lies in its attempt to prevent and reduce mental illness using certain therapeutic approaches. One is to give treatment to preschool children at the earliest stages of emotional disturbance, and at the earliest ages. Another is to fortify and facilitate mental health during a severe life crisis, before an illness has set in. (It has been most gratifying to us that part of this work, facilitation of mourning with families suffering bereavement, was recently replicated as a special project in Chicago.)

As director of the Center's Situational Crisis Service, I am more concerned with the latter therapy. My staff and I work with *psychologically healthy* people who have been victimized by an external life event. I emphasize those words because so many people, including some who come to us, are still skeptical if not antagonistic to psychiatric treatment. Erroneously they believe only psychotic or deeply neurotic people need or could benefit from psychiatric intervention, or fear that all treatment must be long-term, intensive, or costly. Actually, situational crisis intervention usually runs no more than ten to twenty sessions; frequency of sessions is determined by the family and therapist together; and fees at the Center are on a sliding scale, according to ability to pay. Our aim is to educate families (and the community) to what is expectable following an acute stress, to strengthen healthy, growth-promoting reactions, and to encourage the sharing of feelings in critical situations. We try to acknowledge the dangers inherent in severe stress and to increase the opportunities and options available for adaptation.

We feel we are beginning to be successful. In 1965, our first year, only 32 people were seen by all four of the Center's divisions. In 1975, 334 people comprising 112 families were seen by the Situational Crisis Service alone. Equally important, back in 1965 the average interval between the datable stress and referral to the Center was 1,000 days; in 1976 that interval dropped to only 60 days, with referrals for parental death, suicide, and rape usually occurring within twenty-four hours. And in the past several years, an increasing number of families have been coming in upon diagnosis of a potentially fatal illness, or at the time a critical change such as separation, divorce, or major surgery is being considered. Most gratifyingly, more than 20 percent of the people who now come to the Center for preventive intervention have been referred by family or friends who themselves received help there. We have learned, and they have learned, that there is little so dreadful that it cannot be talked about, and that what we can talk about we have a chance to master.

There are two situational crises with which this book does not deal. One is natural disasters, which, as previously noted, bear more on communal considerations than those of family crisis. The other is unemployment, a crisis of the '70s in which I have not yet had sufficient clinical experience. I have also excluded such expectable and developmental turns of life as birth, marriage, children leaving home, relocation, and retirement.

Much of what I have learned at the Center is not difficult to share. Situational crisis intervention is a type of psychological first aid. Unlike standard psychotherapy or psychoanalysis, which addresses itself to intrapsychic problems, and thus requires long-term or intensive treatment, situational crisis intervention is designed to prevent problems before they start, or before they become entrenched as part of the character of the stressed individual or family. If taken seriously at the moment of vulnerability, the danger or stress can be transformed into a healing, growth-promoting experience.

The ancient Chinese were evidently aware of this process, for in their language they combined the characters for "danger" and "opportunity" to form the ideogram for "crisis." Thomas Paine was pragmatically assured when he wrote, "Danger and deliverance make their advance together," and Shakespeare expressed it most eloquently: "Out of this nettle, danger, we pluck the flower, safety."

No Time to Mourn, No Time to Mend

2

A hundred years ago death was considered an expected, natural part of the life cycle. The experience of a loved one's passing was shared by old and young, male and female, families and friends. In this century, however, as science has provided us with increasingly wondrous ways to thwart death and prolong life, death has come to be regarded as an unwelcome and often willfully unrecognized stranger. We try to close our minds to its existence, to shun its effects. In the Victorian era, a time when death was still accepted as a natural experience, socially uniting for its survivors, the great unspeakable subject was sex. Today sex is out in the open, a topic of enormous public awareness, and death has become the obscenity.

Yet death is around us more than ever. We cannot read a newspaper, watch television, or live in a community without the fact of death invading our consciousness. Constantly we are made aware of people dying—from illness, accident, or human violence; dying suddenly or slowly. No matter how hard we try to deny the reality, we cannot change it. What we can do is find better, less painful ways to live with it.

We know intuitively, and researchers over the past twenty years support the impression, that the way in which we deal with death depends, in large measure, on the circumstances of death. It is sad but not tragic when a ninety-one-year-old grandmother dies peacefully in her sleep. It is more than tragic, it is an outrage against nature, when a child dies before his parents or grandparents. And it is tragic, frightening, and overwhelming when a parent of young children dies. Suicide is especially confounding (so much so that a separate chapter of this book will be devoted to it). Indeed, the less understandable and "reasonable" the way of death, the less able we are to cope with it and to do the work of mourning.

"The work of mourning" may seem a strange phrase, but it is appropriate and useful to our purposes, a term that can help us organize our thinking and recognize our feelings. Death is an *event* that results in a *state of bereavement* among the survivors, which in turn requires the *work of mourning* so they may continue to live in the least stressful, most gratifying way. And it is indeed work—painful, hard, exhausting, and often seemingly endless. It entails the remembering and reviewing of countless memories of, and interactions with, the person who died. A crucial requirement is that *all* types of memories and interactions be recalled and shared by the bereaved; not just the loving, warm, and joyful ones, but also those that were characterized by anger, sadness, disappointment, and hurt. Unless we can recall such memories of pain and conflict, we are idealizing the dead and running the risk of devaluing, even rejecting, our relationships with the living, which can then frustrate and deprive us of the gradual and meaningful development of new relationships. The more we idealize the dead, the more we have lost not only the loved one but also our own most vital sense of self-esteem and self-love.

The Morgans came to see me the day after their nine-year-old son, Pete, had been killed in a diving accident. Referred to the Center by their clergyman in the course of making their funeral arrangements, they came because in the less than twenty-four hours since Pete's death, in the throes of shock and despair, they had begun to lose faith in their own judgment, and in each other.

Carl Morgan, tight-lipped and stiff, said he couldn't believe it. Pete had been diving since he was five, it just wasn't possible! Janet Morgan burst into tears. "But if you hadn't pushed him so much he wouldn't have gone swimming yesterday, he'd have gone biking with his friends and he'd still be alive." She went on to tell me about Pete, what a wonderful, handsome, affectionate, fun-loving boy he was. "He never hurt anyone, he just loved life. And now he's dead. It should have been me, he had his whole life in front of him. He was so young. Oh, my God! I can't believe it."

Mr. Morgan was shaking his head. "I didn't push him, I didn't! He loved swimming, you know that. We saw him afterward, there wasn't a mark on him. They said he slipped when he went off the board and broke his neck, but there wasn't a mark on him. I never pushed him, never. Good God, what am I going to do? Sam's only five, he can't understand why Pete doesn't come home. What can I tell him? And Sally, who's eleven, started to scream when we told her and locked herself in her room and won't come out. Yesterday we were a family, a pretty happy family, and today we have nothing. Nothing!"

I listened for a long time, and then we talked. We talked about how death makes us feel helpless, and how when it's so hard to understand why a loved one dies we look for someone or something to blame. And when there's no one and nothing to blame in such a sudden, freaky accident, we blame ourselves and each other. I said, "This is happening to both of you now. It's important for you to realize you're sharing the same grief. But instead of holding on to each other you're pushing yourselves apart. Sally is locking herself away from you in her hurt, and Sam is lost in all the confusion."

Carl Morgan began to slump in his chair and tears rolled down his face. He turned to his wife and she reached out, took his hand, and held it to her cheek. "Oh, Jan, how can we bear it?"

"By doing what you're doing now," I said, "by touching each other and sharing your feelings. And as you both are sharing your feelings now, so you need to share with your children—as much as they need it. A moment ago you said 'Today we have nothing,' but the truth is you have each other, Sally, and Sam. And it's precisely because Pete died that you all need each other more urgently and desperately than before."

Janet Morgan nodded, "But it's so hard for us to believe Pete's dead. I don't believe it, I keep thinking he'll come bombing into the kitchen as he always did, throw his stuff on a chair, dive into the refrigerator, and yell, 'Hi, Mom, I'm starved!' If I can't believe it, and I'm an adult, how can the kids believe it?"

"You can help the kids by telling them what you've told me. That it *is* hard to believe, that you don't *want* to believe it, but you *have* to believe it, as sad and painful as it is. And beyond sharing your feelings, there are practical actions you can take to help the children both to accept the reality and to begin the work of mourning. What would you say is your first such opportunity?"

Mr. Morgan said, "We thought Sally should come to the funeral because she's old enough to understand, but we hadn't thought of taking Sam. Now I'm not so sure he should be excluded."

Mrs. Morgan nodded. "He should stay close to us, but I'm worried that he'll be confused and upset by what he sees."

"He could be," I said, "but if he's prepared *in advance* for what he will experience, and if you are both near to answer his questions and hold him, he'll be neither surprised or shocked. In fact, seeing Pete in the coffin will help confirm the reality of his brother's death. And seeing family and friends sad and upset will help him know it's okay, it's safe, to have these feelings. No matter what you do or don't do, Sam will be upset. But what you do can help him cope with being upset."

Over the next four months I saw all the Morgans together once a week and had other occasional sessions with the parents to discuss their problems and to offer some parental guidance. The family shared with each other their memories of Pete; they cried, laughed, argued, and did the work of mourning together. During this time each of them developed temporary symptoms: Sam had nightmares of Pete not being able to breathe in the grave, and of Pete coming back to "get" him. His parents and sister were able to help him understand that dead people don't breathe or eat or move around, and gradually the nightmares subsided. When Sally began to overeat, we were able to help her see that she was trying to fill up the empty feeling that came from missing Pete. She also had several minor accidents and was helped to understand that this was her way of punishing herself for what she told us were all the "mean" things she had said to Pete. Both parents had some sleeping difficulties, and Mr. Morgan developed transitory head and neck pains, which disappeared shortly after Mrs. Morgan told him in a family session, "I guess that's your way of remembering how Pete died."

The Morgan family was essentially a healthy, well-functioning family before Pete's sudden death, and because of their health and with the assistance of brief therapeutic intervention, they have continued to live happily and grow well. I have seen them once a year now for the past seven years. Sam is sixteen and Sally twenty-two. Mrs. Morgan experienced some anxiety when Sam turned nine, Pete's age when he died, but she was aware of the connection and was able to deal with her tendency to overprotect Sam. Her husband gave her considerable support in encouraging Sam to develop appropriately. Pete has not been forgotten over the years, nor will he ever be forgotten. But the Morgans know they are a family.

Mr. Gray came to the Center three weeks after his wife was killed in an automobile accident. He came not so much because he was flooded with grief (though he certainly was) but because he couldn't handle his rage or his children's behavior. Marion Gray had been killed when another car blew a front tire, went out of control, and crashed into her car, smashing it head-on into a tree. At first Mr. Gray's anger appeared directed toward that "stupid son-of-a-bitch idiot who never should have been allowed behind the wheel of a car." He said that it had been three weeks and he still couldn't believe she was dead. It was so sudden—out of nowhere. His wife had been wiped out as if she had never existed. But her presence was everywhere: visible in Lucy's still pudgy, twelve-year-old face; in the quickness of Jay's movements, made even jerkier by adolescence; by his wife's clothes hanging in the closet, her shower cap askew over the bathtub faucet; by the cloying odor of a still-wet clay head she had been sculpting in the corner of the basement.

Mr. Gray snuffed out his cigarette angrily. "I hate that damn smell. My hobby's furniture making and my workshop's in the basement too. We'd argue about her sculpting at home because the odor got into everything. Then she'd get mad and say it was all right for me to have my priorities but it wasn't all right for her to have her priorities. Only it went too far. She'd never forget to shop for fresh clay, or wire, or tools, but she'd forget to get my Earl Grey tea, or Jay's pants at the cleaners. She even stopped taking Lucy to her music lesson, saying she was too busy and Lucy was too lazy to ride her bike there. Marion and I argued so much lately, I was angry at her so often—and now I'm furious with the kids. But Jay is so damned irresponsible. He's never home when I need him, sometimes he's not even home for dinner and I don't know where the hell he is! And Lucy has turned into a crybaby. She barely cried when Marion died, but now she cries over nothing—or yells over something stupid and un-important. It's just ridiculous! It's gotten so I can't concen-trate on my work, and in architectural design one slip and the whole thing has to be done all over again."

Arguments, yelling, slamming doors—not only did it seem that no one cared that Mrs. Gray had died, it was as if everyone suddenly hated everyone else. "Why can I only remember the bad times?" Mr. Gray cried out. "They weren't all bad. Not at all."

Marion Gray had been a good person, a caring wife and mother. She'd had a special ability to make people laugh, to mock her own failings so transparently that her husband would hug her and say, "Oh, that's not so!" and they would giggle together at the old game. It was true that in the past year she no longer drove Lucy to her music lessons, but she did spend hours playing the piano while Lucy practiced her flute, and talked with her daughter endlessly about "girl things" when Lucy got moody.

Mr. Gray shook his head and absently rubbed the back of his neck. "Marion still knew when I got down or worried, maybe not quite as often as before, but most of the time. She'd rub my neck and leave funny or loving notes pinned to the shirt I was going to wear, or taped to the bathroom mirror for me to find when I went in to shave. We had so many good and special things. Why are they so hard for me to remember now? Why am I so furious?!''

I assured him that his anger was entirely appropriate. "We are always angry when someone we love dies. But modern society still dictates that we 'must not speak ill of the dead.' When such thoughts come unbidden and unwelcome we feel frightened, and often ashamed. The more anger, disappointment, and ambivalence that exist in our relationship with a spouse, the more frightened we are at our angry memories when our spouse dies. So we defend ourselves against our fear as coaches and politicians recommend—'The best defense is a good offense.' We get angry. We feel, 'She abandoned me!' 'Look at what she left me with!' 'How could she do this to me!' even as we recognize logically that it couldn't be her fault, her doing. Mr. Gray, death makes us feel helpless; it also regresses us temporarily, no matter how mature or adult we are, to a much earlier stage of development when we believed everything happened because it was wished for or wanted. This may not seem logical or reasonable, but it's virtually universal in our culture—and it is understandable.''

For the Gray family there were many "reasonable" grounds for having been angry at Mrs. Gray, as there are in nearly all human relationships. The Grays had had more opportunities for friction than most families because all of them had been "doing their own thing," often inconveniencing or interfering with their "togetherness." While it was appropriate for Jay and Lucy often to be angry at their mother, especially since adolescence is the time for children to challenge parental authority, they had been robbed of the time to work out and master their feelings. Their mother was no longer there to fight back—to make demands, give support, and love them—so they had to fight with each other.

The suddenness and violence of Marion Gray's death had left her family stunned and raging. (Since sudden accidental death is usually violent and often mutilating, an additional burden of dealing with the horrifying aspects of the death is placed upon the survivors.) They'd had no time to adjust to the reality of her death, and no time to say their last good-byes. Both the reality and the feelings about the reality needed to be shared and dealt with by each family member.

It took longer to facilitate the work of mourning with the Grays than with the Morgans. I saw the Grays together twice a week for a period of eight months. During that time they came to recognize that they were sharing many of the same feelings, though in harsh and maladaptive ways. They were aided in acknowledging, then accepting their anger, and with this acceptance each of them became free to remember the loving, happy, close memories as well. By the end of their therapy, Jay, Lucy, and Mr. Gray were able to reconstruct themselves as a family of individuals with separate wants, needs, and concerns.

On the occasion of a follow-up session with the family four years later, I was pleased to learn that Mr. Gray was about to marry a woman who genuinely enjoyed Lucy and Jay. Lucy was a senior in high school and had decided on a career as a flutist; she had been accepted at a college noted for its musicology. I'm sure it was more than coincidence that Mr. Gray's fiancée was a violinist and an active member of their community orchestra. Jay was about to start graduate work in engineering and, as he wryly told me, "Maybe I can invent a crash-proof car." Then he grinned and added, "I'd really like to design a radically new type of city transportation so that cars would become obsolete."

What particularly gratified me was seeing the actualization of a theory in which I had long believed. Anger is not bad or maladaptive in and of itself. It is a manifestation of energy that demands expression. How that energy is expressed determines the individual's ability to cope productively. Jay was able to apply his aggressive energy to the mastery of his long-term professional goals with a remarkably appropriate ambition, just as Lucy was able to invest hers in nurturing and polishing her musical skill. As Mr. Gray came increasingly to terms with his own anger, he found himself free to reinvest his energies in his work and his hobby, and his fiancée. The Grays had accomplished their work of mourning well.

When death comes by sudden unexpected illness—when it occurs in seconds, minutes, or hours—it can bring with it many of the problems of accidental death. Perhaps the major difference is that such deaths are hardly ever mutilating, thus horror is rarely an issue. What is critical is the overwhelming sense of disbelief that someone alive and healthy minutes or days before could suddenly die. It just doesn't seem possible.

The Claytons came to the Center a week after Meg, their three-month-old daughter, succumbed to "crib death," perhaps the most difficult or demoralizing loss for a family to bear.

Parents who have lost a child to Sudden Infant Death Syndrome, the professional name for "crib death," have one of the highest rates of separation and divorce of any group in the country. On the surface it would appear that losing a baby would be less demolishing than losing an older child, a child whom the parents had learned to know and love. It seems logical that one's sense of loss would be in direct proportion to the length of time a child is loved and cared for. The unconscious, however, does not operate logically, and a large part of our feelings is determined by unconscious factors. A baby is totally dependent upon its parents for food, warmth, comfort, love, and survival. As parents we accept our responsibility and desire to nurture, protect, and love our baby. We may get tired or irritable because of its demands, but we delight in and feel fulfilled by our baby's contented gurgle after feeding, by its smile and vanishing tears as we come into view, by the feel of the baby snuggling in our arms. And in turn we invest and endow our baby with all our dreams, hopes, and wishes. Our baby becomes the embodiment of our future.

The Claytons had been referred to us by a nurse in the emergency room where they had rushed Meg the afternoon she died, but Bill and Wendy Clayton had been too stunned to hear the nurse's recommendation. Six days later their pediatrician had urged them to bring Mike, their four-year-old son, to us because he had begun wetting his pants, could not let his mother out of sight for an instant, was terrified to sleep alone, and had begun "crying over nothing."

The story the Claytons told was painfully typical. Meg had been a healthy, happy, wonderful baby. She had been put into her crib for a nap after lunch. She had cooed for a few minutes before falling asleep, and Wendy Clayton had adjusted the blanket and told Mike to play quietly with his toys so as not to wake his sister. Then Mrs. Clayton went into the bathroom to wash her hair. Ten minutes later she peeked into the children's room, saw Meg asleep, and asked Mike if he wanted to keep her company while she dried her hair. Mike shook his head and said he was too busy building a garage even bigger than the one Daddy worked at. For the next hour Mrs. Clayton busied herself fixing her hair, folding laundry, making a phone call, and then went into the kitchen to make a cup of coffee for herself and to slice an apple for Mike. She was surprised to find Meg still asleep when she reentered the bedroom. Meg rarely napped long in the afternoon; this was her most active playtime. Mike was standing by the edge of the crib watching Meg. Wendy Clayton bent over the crib and saw how quiet Meg was. She picked her up—Meg wasn't breathing. She screamed, "Michael, my God! What did you do!" She turned Meg upside down and began pounding on her back, but Meg still did not breathe. Mike was crying and trying to say something, but she told him to shut up—"I have to hear the baby's heartbeat!"—but there was none. She tried mouth-to-mouth resuscitation, as she had seen it done once on TV, but still Meg did not breathe. She gathered Meg in her arms, grabbed Mike, and raced to the hospital. She refused to let the emergency-room team separate her from Meg. Leaving Mike in the waiting room, she watched the doctors and nurses try to revive Meg. After what seemed hours a doctor turned to her, "I'm sorry. I'm so sorry. We tried everything we could. I'm so terribly sorry." Someone came over and sat her down. "You'll want to call your husband; shall I call him for you?" The next hours passed in a daze. Dimly she remembered her husband's arrival at the hospital. Confusedly he remembered questions, forms, releases, offers of a sedative, and Mike's sitting frozen and silent on the waiting-room couch, refusing to respond to a pink-uniformed woman trying to play with him.

Bill Clayton said, "We were so confused, so stunned. All I can remember for the next week is a swirl of confusion and that my guts were being torn out. And the questions— Why? How? Why couldn't they help her? Why didn't Wendy . . ."

Wendy Clayton interrupted. "I kept asking myself why I hadn't checked before I did the laundry. Maybe if . . . And the doctors, the autopsy report: no answers, at least none that make any sense. 'Sudden Infant Death Syndrome,' 'crib death.' "

Bill Clayton clenched his fist. "All they told us was 'nothing.' They said it was *nothing* we did, *nothing* anyone did, *nothing* we didn't do. They said she didn't smother in the blanket, didn't choke on her lunch. They didn't know what caused it, but said they were 'working on it.' And they all said they were sorry. What the hell good is 'sorry'!" he shouted. "What good are answers that aren't answers?"

Wendy Clayton began to cry. "I can't even take good care of Mike anymore. I tried to apologize for screaming at him—for yelling 'What did you do?'—but he just turned away, and a few minutes later he wet his pants.''

"What I did was worse," Bill Clayton said. "I was the one who got mad and spanked him for being a baby. I'm the one who really took it out on Mike. And oh Jesus, the pressures! We're being smothered. Our parents, our friends, our neighbors, they're drowning us in food, in questions and advice.''

"My best friend told me I can have another baby," said Wendy Clayton. "She thought that would be comforting. And she said I should stop thinking about Meg because nothing can hurt her now. Bill's mother said I'll be pregnant in three months and I'll forget this ever happened. They want to make me forget. They keep pushing Valium at me to calm my nerves, and they tell me I need to sleep, I'm exhausted. But I can't forget."

Mr. Clayton had shut his eyes. "Wendy can't forget," he said, "I can't forget, Mike can't forget. And Mike's in the middle. People keep telling him to leave Wendy alone, to stop clinging; they tell him he's too old to wet his pants. And then we tell him the same thing; we have no patience with him. My God! I don't know how to act anymore."

I listened without interrupting. There was a good deal I could have said, but it could wait. Bill and Wendy Clayton needed to express their torment, and they needed me to hear them express it.

No malice or cruelty or even insensitivity was intended by anyone in the Claytons' network of family and friends, but their attempt to ease the pain and guilt by urging replacement (a new baby right away), by forgetting and not talking, by avoiding appropriate expressions of emotion, all served to increase the overload of burdens the Claytons were already carrying.

I saw the Claytons as a family twice a week for nine months and then once a week for three more months. Now three years later I see them twice a year. There was a tremendous amount of work to be done—and undone. As with all bereaved families I helped them to share their feelings about the sudden loss of Meg. But that was only the beginning. They needed to know that their feelings were *appropriate and necessary,* not signs of weakness, sickness, or "craziness." As Mike's parents, they needed to understand that he was only four and developmentally in the stage of magical thinking (as are all children until age eight), and thus still not mature enough to know that all the angry, resentful thoughts and wishes he had directed openly or secretly toward Meg were not responsible for her death. They needed to understand how his clinging and fear of being alone at bedtime reflected an age-appropriate anxiety—after all, if Meg died in her sleep, maybe he or Mommy or Daddy would too. And they needed to understand that his wetting was a regression, again age-appropriate, and expectable under acute stress. Young children mourn differently from adults, but they do mourn and they can do most of the work of mourning with the help of the important adults around them. The Claytons learned to respond to Mike's "crying over nothing" by saying that they knew it was hard for a little boy to cry about something so scary as having his sister die. They told him that when a person has a lot of crying feelings inside it's easier to let them out over something like not being allowed ice cream just before dinner, or losing a toy, or getting a tiny scrape on a knee.

As the Claytons became more sensitized to Mike's way of grieving and mourning, they became more aware of the characteristics of their own mourning. Mrs. Clayton was soon able to speak freely about her sense of guilt, and gradually to distinguish her self-accusations as a way of dealing with her sense of helplessness and loss of self-esteem from not having been able to protect and save her baby. But she also turned increasingly away from her husband for love and support—at first stating that Mike needed her full attention now—and it became apparent that she was punishing herself for the loss of Meg before her husband could.

It took many months for this to come out in the open, and when it did it had a liberating effect on both of them. Mrs. Clayton turned to her husband in my office, at last able to confront him, and said, "You really do blame me, don't you?"

Mr. Clayton became utterly still, and I imagined I could hear their heartbeats thumping in the silence. Finally he admitted he had originally blamed her, and despite all he had learned about "crib death," the thought still popped into his head. He apologized for believing her responsible, but then expressed bitterness and anger at how she had changed since Meg's death. She used to be affectionate and sexy, she had cared for him, but now she was only concerned with keeping the apartment spotless and caring for Mike. "It's as if you don't care whether I'm there or not, except when I bring home the weekly paycheck," he exclaimed, and when his wife burst into tears he shouted, "Damn you! Meg was my child too! Don't you think I care! Don't you think I miss her! She was just becoming a person. I was just beginning not only to love her, but to know her. Don't you think I hurt too! You act like you and Mike are the only ones suffering. You are so goddamn selfish I might just as well leave, you probably wouldn't even notice!"

I heaved a sigh of relief. For several months I had been aware of the undercurrents of friction and withdrawal the Claytons were experiencing and inflicting on each other, but all the therapeutic insight in the world didn't mean a thing until the Claytons were ready to deal with the problem themselves. Their outburst was the turning point. At last Wendy Clayton could accept responsibility for turning away from her husband as a defensive reaction to her sense of his blaming her, and Bill Clayton could accept responsibility for not allowing his wife to know how deeply he needed her love and support, and for passively accepting her withdrawal. As both came to recognize the other's pain, they were increasingly able to share the burden and mutually ease it. It took time. The frictions did not disappear instantly; but as the Claytons worked out their marital disharmonies, they worked on their harmonies as well.

It has been three years since Meg's death. A year and a half ago Jeff was born, and the Claytons expressed delight in his birth and some relief that it was a boy, for if it had been a girl they might have fallen into the trap of comparing her with Meg. We spoke right after the birth about the possibility that they might become anxious as Jeff approached the age Meg had been when she died, and when that time came they called me to say that, yes, they were "more irritable than usual," but having been warned that all such anniversary times are difficult, they were "okay." When I saw them at their regular six-month follow-up, they were indeed okay.

There have been families who suddenly lost a baby or young child whom I have not been able to assist adequately. Without exception these have been couples whose interactions before the bereavement were characterized by lack of trust, unresolved angers, or disappointment in each other, and usually who either had not wanted the baby in the first place or were then disappointed in or aggravated by the child. As with all major life changes and crises, the more loving or gratifying the individual or family relationships beforehand, the better able the family is to "pluck the flower, safety."

The Goldens were referred to the Center by a close friend ten days after Mr. Golden had died suddenly of a massive coronary, just one day short of his forty-third birthday. Esther Golden kept saying over and over, "It just isn't fair, it just isn't fair!" She told me that they had had a difficult time their first eleven years together, but that over the past six years their marriage had begun to work out, and in just the last year they had really begun to appreciate each other in ways that made them very happy together. Jon Golden had been a free-lance landscape architect who loved all growing things, most of all his children. He was more interested in making them and his bushes and flowers bloom than in "making money or being a success." He was easygoing, relaxed, and would rather putter around the kitchen, take twelve-year-old Josh fishing, or sit and read poetry with sixteen-year-old Ellen, than race around looking for contracts. Esther Golden, on the other hand, was a hard-driving, highly intellectual woman who had "made it" as the director of a small but very successful management consultant firm. The change in their relationship six years ago had come out of one of their continual bitter arguments.

"No, I can't call it an argument," Esther Golden said. "Jon would never argue. No matter how angry I got or how much I yelled, he never argued back. This time, as I was again trying to push him to make something of himself, he very quietly suggested that perhaps I was the one who wanted to make something of myself and why didn't I go out and try it. I realized he was right, but I was scared. It had been years since I had a real job, and I had no degree in anything that could get me the kind of job I really wanted. Jon encouraged me to go back to school. I did, earned my degree in business administration, found a job, and from that took off like a rocket. I love my work, the challenge, the surprise when my clients find out I'm a woman. The best thing about the change was the way I began to feel about myself. I didn't have to push Jon. The qualities that used to infuriate me about him became the very things I learned to love most about him—his gentleness, his uncritical support, his even, unpressured warmth when I'd get home at night. Even our sex life changed. I don't know if it became so good for me because I wasn't so angry at him anymore and could really enjoy him, or if he felt so good about the change in me that he became more interested, but it was wonderful for the last year and a half. It's just not fair, we had so little time loving and appreciating each other.''

I agreed it was not fair and asked her what had happened when he died and how the children reacted. Esther Golden said, ''Jon died as he lived, gently and quietly. We'd finished dinner and I was on the phone making last-minute arrangements for a small family birthday party I'd planned for the next day. Ellie was doing her homework and Josh was working on a fishing lure he was going to use on the weekend. Jon was in his chair reading Frost and suddenly he just gasped and slumped over. Ellen screamed, Josh jumped up, and I ran to Jon, but he was dead. I tried mouth-to-mouth and Josh was pounding on his father's chest and crying, and Ellie called the police.'' The tears were streaming down her face, and her voice was little more than a whisper as she continued, ''We all went together in the ambulance, but we knew nothing could be done. We knew, but we couldn't believe. On that endless ride to the hospital we kept saying just that, how Jon wasn't the type for a coronary—he wasn't a pressured person, he wasn't overweight, no one in his family had heart trouble, he didn't even smoke! I'm the one who should have had the heart attack, not Jon. It should have been me!''

We talked a long time about her feelings, and about how difficult it was to understand. The autopsy report was very clear. Jon Golden had died when a large artery in his heart burst. He had probably been born with a weak spot, like a bubble on a tire, and it suddenly blew out. There was nothing that could have been done, no way it could have been predicted. When he had gone for his yearly physical and was given an electrocardiogram, just two months before, his doctor had told him he'd probably live to be a hundred. Mrs. Golden was concerned about Josh; she was sure that he, being so much like his father, had a weak spot in his heart too.

I met with Josh, Ellen, and Esther Golden weekly for several months. I saw them as healthy people who had suffered a sudden and totally unexpected bereavement, but people who were coping quite well. All of them had difficulty falling asleep, and Mrs. Golden would wake very early in the morning and be unable to go back to sleep. Josh was having trouble concentrating in class and had begun to play hooky from Hebrew school. Ellen had become unusually irritable and angry with her mother, especially resentful of her mother's frequent tears. During this time we worked on each of their reactive symptoms to reveal them as expectable and adaptive ways of expressing grief. Ellen's anger at her mother, developmentally appropriate in mid-adolescence, was increased by the burden she felt of new responsibilities placed on her since her father's death. She resented the fact that her mother couldn't "take care of everything like a mother should." Overwhelmed by her mother's tearful grief, she tried to dose her own pain by turning away from her mother—directly by avoiding her, indirectly through expressions of anger, Josh's avoidance of Hebrew school (which he had previously enjoyed) was directly related to the ancient Judaic tradition that when a boy reaches thirteen and has his Bar Mitzvah he becomes a man. The many comments from relatives and friends complicated and underscored the tradition even more: "Now, Josh, you will have to be the man of the house and take care of your mother and sister." But the final pressure to "be a man" came from Josh himself. He both wanted that manhood and was frightened by the fantasies through which he anticipated making such a jump into precocious maturity. Here Josh received a great deal of support and reassurance from his mother and his rabbi. Esther Golden told him in no uncertain terms that he was still a boy, he was her son, and *that* was what she wanted him and expected him to be. She added, almost fiercely, that she needed him to be Josh, not Jon. The rabbi confirmed that the Bar Mitzvah is traditional and symbolic and that no thirteen-year-old in our society, no matter how smart or determined, is ready or able to function as an adult.

After several weeks of sessions with the Goldens a dramatic event took place. We were talking about what each one remembered and missed most about Jon Golden and suddenly Josh began to cry and shake his head. Ellen and Mrs. Golden tried to comfort him, but I said I thought Josh had something really troubling him and it would be good if he could talk about it. He whispered that he wanted to talk to me alone, and his mother and sister left the room.

Josh appeared very shaken. Holding tightly to the arms of his chair, he said, "I'm going crazy!"

"What makes you think that, Josh?"

"When you see and hear people who aren't there, that's crazy, isn't it? It's a hallucination, and only crazy people have hallucinations."

"Tell me what you see and hear."

"It's my father. I see my father. When I'm falling asleep or sometimes when I'm waking in the morning I see my father standing in the doorway of my room. He calls to me and tells me to get up."

"Josh, I can see how very frightening this must be for you, but I don't think it's crazy. Tell me, before your father died, did he ever stand in your doorway?"

"Yes, Dad always came in to check on me at night— you know, to pull up the blankets I'd kick off—and he was the one who always woke me in the morning because I sleep right through the alarm."

"What you're telling me makes sense, Josh, and it's not crazy at all. Seeing and hearing your Dad in a familiar situation is one way you have of remembering him, feeling less lonely for him. You don't really believe your father is alive, but you wish he were. What you're calling crazy, what you're seeing, is really a wish. A loving wish and memory that occurs at a time when you are in a state between waking and sleeping. It's a perfectly normal phenomenon, but it's frightening if you don't understand it. You know, it wouldn't surprise me if either your mother or sister has had the same experience, and if they have, they were probably frightened too. Maybe still are. I think it would be very helpful if you were willing to share with them what you told me. Would you?''

Josh nodded and stood up to get his mother and sister. ''Are you sure it's not crazy?''

I smiled. ''Josh, I'm very sure.''

Esther Golden was startled by Josh's experience, but also reassured. She told him that she saw his father many times, usually sitting across from her at the kitchen table. ''You remember, Josh, Dad and I used to drink tea together in the late evening. It was a special talking time for us. I was very frightened the first time it happened, my seeing him like that, but now I find it strangely comforting.'' And then she echoed a point I had made to Josh. ''It's like a dream—or maybe like making a wish come true for just an instant, even while knowing it isn't real.''

This experience turned out to be strengthening for the entire family. It also reinforced my conviction about the importance of having families share not only the realities of the situation, but also their fears, wishes, and fantasies.

Jon Golden's death occurred seven years ago. I still see the family yearly. Ellen is now working in public relations for a large foundation, and Josh is studying ecology at a university. Both like what they are doing and appear to have a gratifying social life. Esther Golden has been seeing a man for the past four years. She doesn't feel quite ready to remarry, but she is increasingly sure she will. Her work continues to please her, but she has learned to pace herself more wisely. While her life isn't precisely as she wants it (the apartment is very empty with both children living elsewhere), she is much happier than she would ever have thought possible.

Any book that deals with death must deal also with dying.

I remember being at a party once where a friend of mine

was discussing his dread of making a long trip by airplane. As his friends either agreed with his nervousness or pooh-poohed it, he said, "You don't understand. I'm not afraid of flying, I'm afraid of crashing!" Everyone laughed, and the subject was dropped. Of course he was afraid of flying. As he confessed to me later, he was obsessed while in a plane with all the things that could go wrong. He was paralyzed by anxious attention to every sound and movement that might bode disaster; he was embarrassed by what he thought others would think of him if they knew he was so terrified; he felt helpless.

My friend's emotions were in many ways similar to those of terminally ill people. The anticipation of dying is a different experience from the event of death. Dying may be a process lasting many months or years; death occurs within an instant. While there is rarely any choice in the timing or manner of death, those of us close to the terminally ill all too often act as if there were also no such choices in the process of dying. We act as if the dying person were already dead—not by callous disregard, but by discreetly curtailing much that was characteristic or otherwise integral to the person's way of life. Such surrender inflicts grievous harm not only on the dying but also on us, the bereaved-to-be.

Alan Craig was referred to the Center nine months after his wife, Jean, had been diagnosed as having stomach cancer. After extensive surgery and chemotherapy, she had had a five-month remission during which time she felt quite well and went back to teaching classical mythology at a local university. Jean Craig had not been told the truth.

At her husband's insistence, and with the full coopera-tion of her physician, Jean Craig had been told she had an ulcer, and that was why she was having so much pain and could not keep anything down. Dr. Howell assured her that when she recovered from the surgery, and if she took her medicine, got plenty of rest, and watched her diet, she'd be just fine. And for five months she did seem fine. Then suddenly she got terribly sick and weak and was rehospitalized. Now, Alan Craig told me, the doctors said it was a matter of hours or days. Jean Craig no longer knew what was going on, she was so heavily sedated.

Mr. Craig was especially worried about his daughter, Mary, who was about to graduate from high school. She had never been told how sick her mother was, and, furthermore, Mr. Craig had contrived to keep her away from the hospital so that she wouldn't have to see how awful her mother looked. He told me that only he and his married son, Ed, knew Jean had cancer. He dreaded calling Ed, who lived two hundred miles away with his wife, Trish, and infant daughter, Ginger, but he knew he must. And he knew that he had to tell Mary.

He told me that he had always been "so bad" with words that Jeannie, who loved to talk, used to tease him about his awkwardness in expressing himself verbally. But, he added, the teasing was always gentle. She admitted that she could never do the simplest arithmetic, while there was nothing he couldn't do with numbers. She would hug him and say, "That's *another* reason we're such a good team!" He began to cry as he told me that just before she got sick again he had given her a pocket calculator and had made a card to go with it. On it was a magician with a magic wand in one hand and a top hat in the other. Popping out of the hat was a scarf that had written on it "Here's a bit of magic to help you come up with the right number. Now maybe you can come up with some magic to help me find the right words when I need them. Love you, Alan."

With tears in my eyes, I smiled and said, "For a man who can't find the right words you seem to find loving ways to express what you feel. But even without magic, we need to work together to help you and everyone in your family find the best ways to deal with and share what's happening now.''

Alan Craig agreed to ask his wife whether she would like to talk with me, explaining that I work with people who are sick and hospitalized. Perhaps she would like a chance to talk to someone who wasn't her doctor or a member of the family. We both wondered if she could do it, considering the amount of sedation she was receiving, but we agreed to give it a try. He also agreed to tell Mary how critically ill her mother was and to bring her, Ed, and Ed's wife, Trish, to see me the following afternoon. I asked him if there were any other family members he felt should be included. He shook his head and told me that all four grandparents were dead, but maybe Jean's sister should come—they had been very close and it was going to be a terrible shock to her. We discussed briefly how he would tell his family about coming to see me; I stressed that my work was with people who had been victimized by something that was out of their control, that he should point out how my job was to keep people psychologically healthy, not to treat the mentally ill. Alan Craig said he had never heard of preventive psychiatry before he was told about the Center, but that he was willing to try anything.

Late that night I got a call from Mr. Craig telling me that his wife had lapsed into coma and had died. He asked if I still wanted to see him and his family, and I told him that it was even more important for them to come in. We changed the appointment time to late afternoon so that he would have time to, as he put it, ''do all the things and make all the arrangements I have to.'' I acknowledged the tremendous pressure on him, but again stressed the need for the entire family to be together and discuss not only what had happened but also how each of them felt about it.

Part of me dreaded meeting with the Craigs. After nearly two decades of working with victims it has not become easier. I have become more skilled, I have learned when to talk and when to listen; I've become a more competent facilitator, and I've learned to accept my own feelings. But it's never easy—and I expect it never will be, for then I would lose what is most crucial for a situational crisis therapist: the ability to demonstrate personally that I can bear painful feelings, that these feelings do not humiliate or disorganize me, or interfere with my productive functioning.

Mr. Craig came in with Mary, Ed, Trish, and his sister-in-law, Brenda Daniels. They looked like a bereaved family: dazed, red-eyed, bent with fatigue, and huddled together—all except Mary. She turned her chair away from her father so that she could barely see him and isolated herself from the family group. Before I could finish introducing myself, Mary began to talk, quietly and viciously.

"I went to see my mother yesterday. As I leaned over to kiss her she opened her eyes and I told her how much I loved her. She whispered so softly I could barely hear her. She whispered that she loved me and was so proud of me, and then she shut her eyes. I stayed with her holding her hand, but she didn't open her eyes or say anything again. That must have been when she went into coma, but I didn't even know that! When I got ready to leave I adjusted the covers and I found this." Mary held up a piece of paper, then crumpled it into a ball and threw it at her father. "Read it, damn you, read it out loud so everyone will know. Now you will all know what *you* wouldn't let me know, what *you* wouldn't let Mom know. You made us all live in agony alone. Maybe someday I'll be able to forgive you for what you did to me, but I'll never forgive you for what you did to my mother!"

Mr. Craig's face drained white. He began to read: " 'My darlings— There has been so much that I have wanted to tell you over the past nine months. I didn't, because I couldn't bear to, and I was afraid to question too much because I must have known the answer all the time—and maybe because I thought you couldn't bear to listen. Probably both . . .' "

Mr. Craig's voice broke and he couldn't go on. Ed took
the paper out of his father's hand and in a quavering voice
continued reading. " 'Now there's no time left to tell you
I'm sorry—sorry for all the time lost, the time angry, the time
I didn't hear, or know, or understand, or wouldn't. Like last
summer, Mary. I guess I wasn't ready for you to be grown up
and independent and so far away. You were ready, but I
wasn't. Or when I wouldn't let you play in the band, Eddie,
for all the silly, overprotective reasons I gave you. Like so
many times, Alan, that now I can never make up to you, and
you can never make up to me. I thought we had so much
time, Alan. I wasted the tiny bit I had left. Did I really ever
let you know how much I've loved you, how loving *you*
made me feel more lovable, and again more loving. I hope
you won't forget me, not as I am when you read this, but as I
was, and as I wish I could have become. I know that each of
you loved me, each in your own special, precious, and sometimes infuriating way, and you must know how I loved each
of you. I wanted to write separately to each of you, even to
tiny Ginger, for when she'll be old enough to wonder—but
no time. I'm not afraid as I thought I would be, as I have been
before. Even the pain is bearable, only the losing you (you
losing me) frightens me. No, wrong word—makes me yearn-
ingly sad, even jealous . . . for you will grow, learn, love,
live, and a piece of me will go with you. I'm so tired, so tired
that dying seems natural rather than inevitable, yet still out-
rageous. Can it be both at once? So many strange feelings,
strange yet peaceful. I need you to remember me, to miss me,
to cry, and to stop crying. I love you. I will miss being me
with you.' "

By now everyone was crying. Mary's brother, aunt, and
sister-in-law had made a circle around Mary, holding, touching, soothing. Mr. Craig put a tentative hand to her cheek.
She wouldn't look at him, but neither did she move away.
Everyone began talking at once. They tried to comfort Mary

and one another. Someone said it was all right to cry, all right to be angry. Someone else said not to be angry, Jean hadn't been angry. Trish said we all did the best we could, even the doctors. No one's fault. Not fair. Good life. Happy most of the time. Too little time. So good. So, so lonely.

I listened and began to pull together everything that was being said and shared and tried to connect it with the letter Mrs. Craig had left. I supported the tears and the loneliness, and the anger. And then I pointed out that they were all doing exactly what Jean Craig had requested them to do: to mourn her and to accept all the "strange" and seemingly contradictory feelings that go with the work of mourning. "I'm pleased you're not isolating each other as you feel you isolated Jean. In her last communication she set a standard of living life, of utilizing time. Your reaching out to one another is the most appropriate tribute you can pay her. You are honoring one of her last hopes—that a piece of her go on with you as you 'grow, learn, love, live.' "

Over the next few months much work was done and many issues were discussed, even debated. The Craigs wondered about the quality of Jean's life in her last nine months. All agreed that the surgery and chemotherapy had given her five months of active, happy, gratifying living; all agreed it could have been happier for her, and them, if they had been able to share their caring and concern. It was agreed that the conspiracy of silence on everyone's part, including that of Jean Craig herself, was a bitterly high price to pay for false comfort. The family shared the difficulty and energy drain caused by the lies and evasions that they all contributed. They gradually learned to forgive themselves and Jean Craig for allowing the conspiracy ever to have come about.

It has been less than a year since Mrs. Craig's death. The work of mourning is not yet completed, it is still being done. Mary has grown close to her father, even though she is living at a college two hours away. Ed and Trish visit Alan

Craig so he can share in the joy of Ginger's growth and delight in being Grandpa. Mr. Craig feels the loneliness and yearning of living alone after nearly twenty-six years with Jean, and he still has not forgiven himself as fully as have his children. But he recognizes his self-directed harshness as "ridiculous" and assures his family that he's "still working on it." Because Mr. Craig had a good marriage and liked the feeling of being a loving husband, it is highly probable that he will remarry. He says he is no "swinger," and that it's hard learning all over how to call someone for a date. But he is learning.

The question "What does one tell the dying patient?" has become a major focus of interest in the last decade. I question the question. It matters less what one *tells* a dying person than how well one *listens*. It matters less what we think someone should know than that we be able to hear what someone needs and wants to know. Some time ago I attended a conference at an excellent teaching hospital. The staff felt justly proud that they were taking a new look at the problem of caring for dying patients and their families, including the problems of the care-givers. They reported they had instituted a new team approach. When diagnosis of a potentially fatal illness was made, a team conference would be called to decide what and how to tell the patient. The team included the physician in charge of the case, the consultant/surgeon, the radiologist, chemotherapist (or other specialist), head nurse, consultant psychiatrist, social worker, clergyman, and one responsible family member. An innovative, creative, sensible approach, but one expert was missing—the patient. All of these highly trained, involved professionals assumed that they knew what was best for the patient. I submit that the collective fund of their expertise and knowledge was formidable, but that only the patient knew what he felt, feared, wanted, and didn't want. The only way to meet the patient's needs is to talk with the patient—not at the patient or for the patient, but *with* the patient. The license to be a physician, nurse, clergyman, social worker, or spouse is not a license to deprive a patient of the right of choice.

I am not suggesting that in order to assure someone of his rights that we use truth as a club. When Jean Craig told Alan she was afraid she was going to die, he should not have responded ''That's right, you will '' and dropped the subject. That would have been brutal—and it is precisely to protect people from such brutality that we conspire and lie as we do. What I am suggesting is that it would have been helpful to acknowledge to Jean what she already knew, felt, and observed; to have allowed and encouraged her to ask questions, express fears, and get answers as *she* needed them. It is no more helpful to talk away all hope prematurely than it is to instill false hope. It takes enormous courage *to go where the patient is psychologically,* partly because that means the patient will then know where *we* are. And where we are depends on at least two personal variables—how we ourselves view death, and the quality of the relationship we have had with the dying person.

How we view death is an extremely complicated psychological, sociological, and religious issue, in many ways determined by previous experience, or lack of it. I am not sure it is possible for anyone not dying to come to terms fully with his or her own death. But experience has shown me that being able to think and feel and talk about death, including one's own, makes the eventual, inevitable acceptance less frightening. Over recent years—as part of what would seem to be a healthy trend away from the taboo against open acknowledgment of death—over two thousand courses in ''death education'' have been established in universities, colleges, and high schools. Recently, even some grammar and nursery schools have considered integrating death into the curriculum, a consideration more disturbing to adults than to children, who already seem to know more than most adults like to believe they do. Teaching about death may well excite the same sort of resistance as was encountered by the teaching that the earth revolves around the sun, and by the theory of evolution. But such acquisition of knowledge is what has advanced the progress of our species, and I believe it is the responsibility of educators, at home and at school, knowledgeably to assist students in understanding all aspects of life, including death.

There is also an apparent contradiction between the quality of the relationship we have with the dying person and our ability to do the work of mourning well enough to accept completely the reality of the loss. As implied and illustrated earlier in this chapter, the more loving and gratifying the relationship, the more easily (but not less painfully) we can accept the loss, and the more completely we can continue our own lives. The more conflicted, angry, or disappointing the relationship, the more difficult it is for us to accept the loss, and the harder it is to form new and rewarding relationships.

One of the ways we have of easing our sense of loss is to take into ourselves some part of the lost person. If we remember that person as essentially warm, loving, humorous, creative, or admiring, we tend to adopt those traits or abilities. If what we remember was cold, rejecting, guilt-provoking, hostile, or frightening, we tend to adopt those traits. Indeed, the guiltier we feel about what we did to, or didn't do for, the dead person, the more punishing, harsh, and crippling are the traits we assume. It has to be said that much in the processes of identification with the lost person is not conscious, so we are often unaware of why we feel as we do. And what does stay within our awareness generally causes us less discomfort. If, for example, a widow remembers that her husband used to enjoy seeing her in yellow, she might consciously begin to wear yellow more often. It would sadden her that he was not there to see her, but she would also be remembering his pleasure and feel closer to him. If a child were reminded how much Grandpa used to like tending his tropical fish, the child might adopt the hobby and so feel less lonely for Grandpa. If a close friend had been particularly fond of jazz, playing jazz records might ease that friend's loss. Even adopting a loved one's angers or irritations (directed outward, toward anything from crabgrass to stupid drivers to injustice) could be comforting. Should we somehow not be aware of such positive and adaptive identifications, someone usually points them out to us: "Hey, I didn't know you liked jazz so much," or "When I came in, it was almost like Chip was here!" and the connection is made. But when the connection is not primarily loving, when it is harsh and rejecting, we do not wish to adopt identification. We deny and repress it; then it leaks out in maladaptive behavior.

It had been only sixteen days since five-year-old Bud Putnam had entered the hospital, but the puffy redness of his mother's huge green eyes belied the brief span of time. Betty Putnam's hand shook as she accepted a cigarette from her husband, Hal, whose slumped posture and ashen face reflected his own sense of helpless defeat.

"It's all happened so fast," said Betty Putnam. "Three weeks ago Buddy returned from a birthday party complaining of an upset stomach and a headache. We had all just gotten over a bout of the flu and I thought I had let him out of bed too soon and he was having a relapse. He kept stumbling as I took him upstairs, and he said he had to vomit. I figured he'd had too much junk to eat at the party. Neither Hal nor I were very concerned. Then we were up with him most of the night as he kept vomiting and complaining of a headache. In the morning he was exhausted and fell asleep. When he woke up he still complained of a terrible headache, and when he tried to get to the bathroom he walked as if he were drunk. I called our pediatrician and he said it sounded like the flu and told me to give Buddy the Compazine suppositories to control the nausea and vomiting and to try to get him to drink some Coke in small sips. By the following day he was no better and I took him to see Dr. Fortus. I guess that's when the nightmare began.

"Fortus is a calm, gentle, very easygoing man, and kids really love him. He examined Buddy and suddenly he wasn't calm anymore. He called his nurse, told her to take Bud into the waiting room and to stay with him. Then he said he wanted us to take Buddy to a pediatric neurologist for a consultation. He said that he wasn't sure, but he was afraid that Bud might have a brain tumor. He assured us that Dr. Holt was the best consultant in the East and that she had a wonderful way with kids. Before we could even ask, he told us that there was no way of knowing without extensive tests whether or not there was a tumor and, if there was, what kind of tumor. He tried to be reassuring, but we both knew then."

Betty Putnam started to sob and her husband finished the story for her in a dry, beaten voice. "We took Bud to see Dr. Holt, who immediately hospitalized him. Tests were done, dozens of tests—X rays, scans, blood, urine, tests we'd never heard of, some with names we couldn't even pronounce. Dr. Holt urgently recommended immediate surgery. Yes, there definitely was a tumor, it was believed to be malignant but treatable. She was very hopeful. Sure she was hopeful, Buddy isn't her son! But we agreed to the surgery. They made it clear we had very little choice!"

Betty Putnam went on to describe how she and her husband took turns staying with Bud. The hospital was a good one; they put a cot in Bud's room so one of them could stay with him all night. "But Buddy's only five, he doesn't understand what's going on. He doesn't know why he isn't feeling better, why people keep sticking needles into him, why he has a tube in his arm, why they make him walk when he is so dizzy. He won't eat, he doesn't even look at his favorite toys, and he refuses to talk—even to me. Except that he cries 'Mommy! Mommy!' in his sleep. It's as if they not only took out the tumor, they took out all his spirit. He's not just scared, he's so sad we can't reach him. Dr. Fortus told us that your Center knows how to help little children who have cancer, but what can you do? They removed most of the tumor, now he has to have cobalt treatments and chemotherapy—what can you do about that? Can you stop his hair from falling out? Can you take away his nausea? Can you take away his sadness? How can you stop our nightmare?''

I acknowledged there was nothing I could do to change the reality of Buddy's illness or of the treatment necessary to prolong his life, but there was a great deal that I *and they* could do to help Buddy cope with that reality in less frightened, less sad and passive ways. I asked them to let me see Buddy in the hospital and to prepare him for my visit by telling him that I was a woman who worked with children who were sick and in the hospital, that I understood about the worries and feelings kids have. The Putnams agreed but insisted that I not tell Buddy he had cancer or that he might die. I assured them I would tell Buddy nothing, that I would listen and would discuss only what *he* wanted to talk about. I suggested strongly that Buddy knew more about what was happening to him than any of us wanted him to know, and not encouraging him to express what he already knew (and feared) was imposing an additional stress on him. I asked both parents to be in the room with me when I met with Buddy so that he would not have to deal with still another stranger without the support of his family.

I met Buddy the next afternoon. Propped up in his hospital bed he looked withdrawn, frail, and thin. His large green eyes looked huge in a pale face made tiny by the huge swath of bandages covering his head. He refused to look at me as I sat on the edge of his bed and his parents introduced me. I acknowledged it must be hard to meet still another stranger, especially when he wasn't sure I wouldn't do something to hurt or scare him. He glanced at me and quickly looked away. Since most young children rarely discuss their feelings directly, but will express them through the medium of play and toys, I picked up a piece of Play-Doh from the table. I began rolling it in a ball as I reminded him that I wasn't there to examine him or stick needles in him, but to help him with his scary, sad feelings. Buddy was watching my hands roll the Play-Doh. Suddenly he ordered, "Make me a bunny!" I smiled and told him I wasn't a very good artist, but I would try. I took another piece of the Play-Doh and made the bunny's head. I added paws, a tail, eyes, nose, mouth, whiskers, and finally bunny ears. Buddy was watching me carefully. Suddenly one Play-Doh ear flopped over. Buddy became rigid, his stare fixed on the flopped-over ear. I asked, "Buddy, did the bunny's ear flop over because it wanted to, or is the bunny sick?" Buddy looked at me and said, "The bunny is sick. The bunny is very sick. They are going to take him to the hospital and stick needles in him and take pictures of him and strap him on a table and cut open his head, and put him in buzzing things, and stick things up his bottom. That bunny is so sick."

"Buddy, how does the bunny feel about being sick and having all those things done to him?"

"He's scared, he's scared that one of those buzzing things or one of those needle wires are going to kill him dead. And no one will get him out of the hospital. Superman would, but the bunny doesn't know where he is. He's mad too. The nurses give him food he doesn't like. He won't eat it. And they make him wear a girl's nightgown and he hates that. That bunny's got lots of trouble—just like me."

I nodded at the Putnams, who were sitting in shocked silence. "Buddy, I'm so glad you could tell me how scared and mad the bunny feels. Do you think it would make the bunny feel better if he knew what those buzzing things and needle wires really were? If he knew that they wouldn't kill him dead? And if he could get some food he liked and could wear his own pajamas?''

Buddy smiled. Then he took the bunny out of my hand and whispered in its ''good'' ear. He nodded and shook his bandaged head several times and carried on a long whispered conversation with the bunny. Finally he said, ''Mrs. Kliman, the bunny wants chocolate ice cream and a grape jelly sandwich, but *no butter!* And he wants his superman pj's, and he wants to see Pammy right now.''

I told Buddy that his mommy, daddy, and I could talk to the hospital staff and probably get what the bunny wanted, but I didn't know who Pammy was. Betty Putnam interrupted to say, ''Pammy is Buddy's sister. She's only seven and we didn't think we should bring her here. She knows Buddy's sick, but that's all.''

''But I miss her, Mommy, I want to see Pammy and I bet she wants to see me. I promised her that she could borrow my water pistol, but I want to show her how to use it so she won't break it.''

I told Buddy I understood how important it was for him to keep his promise and to show his sister how to use his water pistol. To his parents I explained how, when a child is sick and feels helpless about all the things that are being done to him, it is terribly important for him to control as much as possible so he is not overwhelmed by all the things he can't control. I added that I thought it very important for Buddy to see his sister, and for Pammy to see him, stressing that what children imagine is often more frightening than the reality. I turned back to Buddy and told him again how glad I was to meet, talk, and play with him, and asked if he would like me to come back again. He said, ''Tomorrow?'' and I grinned. ''No, Buddy, not tomorrow, but I'll come back in two days. In the meantime I'll talk with Dr. Fortus and ask him to explain to you exactly what the buzzing things and needle wires are, and I'll ask him to answer any other questions you have as well."

Dr. Fortus believed as I do that one should explain as much as possible to patients when they ask questions—even very young, very sick patients—and he did a brilliant job. When I arrived at the hospital two days later, Buddy was busily engaged in explaining to Pammy what a cobalt machine was, how IVs put food and medicine directly into his blood so that his stomach didn't get "icky"—and how to reload a water pistol.

Pammy had questions, too. She wanted to know what a tumor was. Buddy told her it was something that grew in his brain, that made him walk "funny" and have "bad headaches." He said that the doctors took it out, and the cobalt machine and medicine "would keep it out." Pammy said it sounded like Buddy had a weed in his brain. Buddy laughed, "That's silly, Pammy! My brain isn't made of grass."

I said, "It's true your brain isn't made of grass, but Pammy has a good idea. If you think of the tumor as a weed, then the operation was like pulling out a weed, and the cobalt and medicine are like the chemicals that we put on the grass to keep out the weeds and make the grass grow better." Buddy became thoughtful. "But sometimes the weeds keep coming back and the grass gets killed." My stomach lurched and I saw the Putnams clutch each other's hands. "That's true, Buddy, and that's a very scary thought, but if the gardeners are very good and watch the grass very carefully, they often can keep away the weeds and keep the grass healthy for a long time. You have very good doctors and nurses and a lot of people who care very, very much about you. They will work very hard to keep your tumor away and keep you healthy. Sometimes they will have to do things that you won't like and that may make you mad, but they will have to do them to keep you healthy. It's okay for you not to like it, it's okay for you to get mad and to tell them. It's no fun being in a hospital, and you don't have to pretend it is . . . but you have to work hard to get better, and it's good there are so many people here to help you.''

After the initial phase of postsurgical recovery and cobalt treatment, Buddy appeared in good shape. He was put on maintenance doses of chemotherapy, which he tolerated well. After his hair fell out he refused to wear a wig, but he accepted a helmet "just like football players wear," and he wore it proudly. He soon learned which headaches would respond to Tylenol and which were going to become severe enough to require a shot. Both parents learned how to give Buddy his shot and to accept his judgment as to when he needed it.

Buddy returned to school six weeks after his surgery. Betty Putnam had spoken to his kindergarten teacher and she had prepared the class for Buddy's return. He fielded such questions as "What happened to you?" "Did it hurt?" "Why're you wearing a helmet? You don't ride a motorcycle!" Once having accepted the helmet, he refused to take it off until *all* his hair grew in. In fact, he would take it off only when he went to bed. Not even Pammy was allowed to see his baldness or his scar.

Over the next three years Buddy lived a full life. He went to day camp and discovered that there were only a few activities in which he could not participate. He learned to swim and ride a bike without training wheels. He did well at school, and while his handwriting was awkward he became a whiz at arithmetic and spelling. Despite occasional absences from school because of severe headaches or checkups, Buddy did very well. He made friends easily with children his own age, and charmed adults with his precocious sensitivity to his own and their feelings—and with his mischievous charm.

My work with the Putnam family during this time was

not limited to Buddy alone. Much attention was paid to Pammy and her anger, jealousy, resentment, and guilt as a result of her brother's "darn tumor." As Pammy was helped to verbalize her feelings, not only to me but also to Buddy and her parents, the Putnams became more attentive to her vulnerabilities and needs. Betty and Hal were themselves helped to enjoy, discipline, teach, and love their son for however long he would live, and not to be trapped into over-indulging or overprotecting him. Priorities were reordered and options were exercised. Despite a limited income, the Putnams arranged a family trip to the Grand Canyon and to Disney World when Buddy was seven. For him it was truly a once-in-a-lifetime experience.

One month after his eighth birthday, Buddy's headaches returned with a vengeance. Palliative medicine no longer had any effect on the pain, and soon even the shots were ineffective. Within several days Buddy was paralyzed. He experienced difficulty breathing and was rehospitalized. I visited him that first evening in the hospital. After all, by this time we were good and trusted friends. I went to hug him and he smiled sadly. "Weird, isn't it—this was the first place I met you and now this is the last place I'll see you."

There were tears in my eyes, and I made no attempt to hide them. "It's really rough this time, isn't it, Super-Bud?"

He whispered, "I remember the first time you called me that—it was when I insisted on riding my bike without training wheels. But I'm not super anymore. I'm so tired."

"Too tired to fight, Bud? You've got a lot of us in your corner."

"I'm too tired. You helped me fight a long time ago, but no one can anymore. Too tired—nothing works anymore. Not worth it anymore. I just want to sleep. Mrs. K., tell Mom and Dad and Pammy to come in a minute. They're in the lounge 'cause I told them I wanted to see you alone a minute. I just wanted you to know I really like you, I like you a lot."

"Bud, I like you a lot, too, a very lot." I kissed him gently and he shut his eyes.

I went to get Bud's family and shared with them that Bud was giving up and I thought that it wouldn't be long now. Betty, Hal, and Pammy went into Bud's room. I sat on the couch and thought about Bud—and ached. Several minutes later Pammy walked toward me. She was crying. I ran to her and she said, "He opened his eyes and said, 'I love you, I really love you,' and then he closed his eyes and we can't wake him."

I returned to his room; a doctor and two nurses were at his bedside. Hal Putnam said, "He's in coma," and began to sob.

Bud was in coma for three days. Three days of waiting, hoping against hope, no longer sure of what was being hoped for. Three days of wishing Bud dead, to end his misery, to end our misery. Three days of helplessness. Once a nurse came to adjust the IV bottle and Betty Putnam screamed at her: "Leave him alone, damn you, stop poking at him. Just leave him in peace!" Hal Putnam took his wife in his arms. "Honey, honey, she's only trying to help. It's not her fault. Just cry, Betty, just cry." She cried, we all cried. And at last what we all knew would be, was. Buddy died. The three years of anticipatory mourning was over. Now Buddy's death was real, and we all had more work to do.

Blame, guilt, rage, sadness, grief, and accusations all had been worked on by the Putnam family over the past three years. But everything had not been worked through sufficiently. Three more months were needed to advance the work of mourning enough for me to stop seeing the Putnams weekly and to put them on follow-up.

It has only been five months since Buddy died, so I can't know how well the Putnams will do. But I am optimistic. Despite the long time it took for Bud to die, most of that time was spent in living—living openly, lovingly, honestly, and fully. For most of that time Bud's illness only minimally interfered with his activities. Unlike many long-term, potentially fatal illnesses, Bud's tumor did not subject him to multiple painful hospitalizations followed by remission, followed by still more hospitalizations. The course of Bud's illness was relatively smooth, and thus his family suffered fewer of those ups and downs that can so erode family relationships. The Putnams were a well-functioning family prior to Bud's diagnosis, psychological first aid was made available and utilized very soon after the onset of the situational crisis, and a strong bonding network of family, friends, and professionals strengthened the family and each of its members.

I wish, both as a clinician and an individual, that we as a society would recognize that when death comes to our loved ones suddenly, horrifyingly, or prematurely, we are *all* subject to stress and its vulnerabilities. I wish we would recognize our victimized status and learn the crucial importance of fully doing the work of mourning. The first step necessary to begin this work is acceptance of the fact: *someone has died.* The rituals inherent in "rites of passage" are age-old and universal. They serve a necessary function of bringing together family and friends at the time of bereavement so that everyone may say a final good-bye, may talk about the deceased, may laugh and cry together within a structure that is supportive and life-promoting. Funerals are thought to honor the dead; in truth they serve the living. It matters not how a funeral is designed—the dead may be buried or cremated, the coffin may be rough pine or velvet-lined mahogany, music may be by Bach or the Beatles, or there may be no music at all. Variations of style are endless and depend only upon the needs and wishes of the mourners. But whether wakes, sitting *shivah,* or condolence calls, all such rituals are acknowledgments of the state of bereavement, and as such have considerable value in facilitating the work of mourning, as well as in affirming that life continues. Those of us who have no time to mourn have no time to mend.

A Sudden Difference

3

EIGHTEEN MILLION HANDICAPPED IN THE UNITED STATES. So read the headline of an article in a highly respected newspaper not long ago. On first glance I was startled by the huge number. On reading into the article, I was appalled, not so much for the eighteen million as for the insensitivity of the writer. The article was well done and scholarly. It referred to "the handicapped" damaged by war, illness, accident, and genetic malfunction. It made a plea to industry to hire "the handicapped" because "the handicapped" are reliable, consistent workers with a low absentee rate. Not once did the article refer to a person, only to a disability or a function. It reminded me of the many times in hospitals when I overheard, "Give me the chart for the melanoma in 604," "Shot time for the pancreas in 519," or "It's a multip, get her to the delivery room fast."

I began to think of how handicapped people have been abused and revictimized for centuries—how lepers were shunned in biblical (and are in current) times; how dwarfs and midgets were treated as playthings in royal courts, and are still treated as freaks in sideshows; how adults pull children away so they can't see the armless or legless on the street. I recalled being instructed by a grade school teacher to "stay away from that Mongolian," a sweet and lonely boy with Down's syndrome who used to hang around the school yard longing for a friend. I thought how fortunate that there was an Annie Sullivan brave enough to find the child locked behind Helen Keller's deafness, blindness, and mutism; and how tragic that there are so few willing to find the men locked behind the wounds and paralyses inflicted by war. And I thought about the handicapped children and adults I knew personally, and had worked with clinically, all of them as gifted, dull, boring, delightful, kind, or mean as people I knew without disabilities. Why then should such people be a special target for our avoidance, our anger, shame, hostility, and fear?

The answer, I believe, lies not so much in our genetic selves as in a complex intermeshing of myth, legend, religion, politics, and developmental psychology. We are born afraid of only two things: being dropped, and sudden loud noises. All other fears are learned by example, through experience, and through age-specific developmental vulnerabilities. For example, babies under eight months have no fear of seeing any person (though they rapidly develop preferences for caretaking people), no matter what that person looks like. Around eight months babies develop a fear of all strangers, but again independent of the stranger's appearance. This stage tends to be short-lived, usually no more than a year (although children may continue to be shy). But then, as children develop and become more aware of their bodies, how their bodies function and are controlled, they also become fearful their bodies may not work, and that they may lose parts of their bodies. At this time most children are frightened to see someone with a limb missing, or even someone in a cast or wearing an eye patch. Still in a stage of magical thinking, they see such a person's handicap as proof that they too will lose a leg or an eye. By around age eight, such magical thinking begins to be mitigated by an increased ability to discriminate between fantasy and reality. Around the same time, however, children also become highly dependent on their peer group; they begin to function not unlike pack animals. Thus again, any stranger, anyone different, excites their anxiety, and this time also their sense of territoriality, their orthodoxy.

Thinking in such developmental terms, it should be easy for adults to understand children's fears at specific ages, to support the reality of the child's intactness and to make clear the irrationality of the child's fears—*unless the adults have never outgrown or mastered their own fears.* All too often, sameness and homogeneity are seen as safety for people who have had little contact with others of different origin, beliefs, even race. Politics and religion, for essentially self-serving reasons, tend to legitimize xenophobia (fear of strangers), as we have seen demonstrated in the persecutions and purges of history—in the martyrdom of the Christians under the Roman Empire, the Spanish Inquisition in the late Middle Ages, and in our own time the Nazi concentration camps and Joseph McCarthy's Communist witch-hunts. Legend and folklore portray people with handicaps as often imbued with magical (and therefore frightening) power, or as embodiments of evil. Of course reasonable and responsible adults don't really believe that trolls lie in wait to attack us, or that the blind have second sight, or that the crippled are being punished for their badness—unless they are under great stress, revert to magical thinking, and thus seek a scapegoat onto which they can project their anger, fear, or sense of helplessness. It was a combination of all these feelings, under the extraordinary strain of World War II, that led us to intern our Japanese-American population in 1942. Unlike the German-Americans or Italian-Americans who resembled us, our Oriental population was alien. Their eyes were shaped differently, their skin was of a different color, even their eating implements were strange. So we panicked and left a legacy of shame from which we have still not recovered. I believe it is this fear of anyone who is different that pushes us into shunning or reviling handicapped people.

Handicaps fall into two categories: congenital, both those obvious at birth and later diagnosed; and those brought on by accident, illness, or exposure to a toxic substance. The problems are different for people in both groups, as are the opportunities for them to live healthily and happily with their disabilities. It is a common misconception that children born with such handicaps as cleft lip and palate, blindness, deafness, or cerebral palsy don't feel different or disabled because they have never known anything different. If only that were true! Their "differentness" may not be perceived for many months, but their inability to make their bodies respond adequately to their needs, wishes, or developmental thrusts is a source of tension long before their first birthday. From the first feeding, the cleft-lip-and-palate baby is frustrated in sucking and swallowing. Blind or deaf babies are frustrated and confused by the lack of visual or auditory clues that orient them to their world. And cerebral palsied babies may be frustrated in attempts to suck their thumb, find their toes, grab a toy, or even to sleep peacefully.

Perhaps most potentially destructive to handicapped children are parental attitudes and responses. As prospective parents we all want and expect perfect babies. And we all harbor some degree of fear that our baby will not be perfect. If it is born with a defect, we are shocked, horrified, and feel guiltily responsible. Not only do we assume it is our (and/or our spouse's) fault, we also believe we have failed as parents. Our baby is not what we expected; it is alien and disappointing. We feel just as defective whenever we see our baby, and what is far worse, just as alien to our baby as our baby feels to us.

Without appropriate medical, social, and psychological support, we tend to see our handicapped baby as the living proof of our inadequacy, or as our punishment. And since none of us can effectively disguise our feelings of guilt, sadness, and anger, they leak out and affect our interactions with the baby. Without support we are vulnerable to abandoning our baby (and our spouse) emotionally, even physically, or we deny and cover up our unacceptable feelings and overprotect our baby, thereby depriving it of a chance to compensate by developing real competence. Either way, our congenitally handicapped baby is doubly victimized, by the burden of having to adapt to the handicap, and by being deprived of the quality of parental nurture necessary to growth and development. We parents also are victimized, and while physiological assistance is frequently available to us, psychological support is much harder to come by.

June and Clark Welles came to see me at the recommendation of both their son's kindergarten teacher and the family pediatrician. They were at their wits' end. Gordie had changed from "a sunny, super li'l fella . . . sometimes a little mischievous," into "an angry, defiant, impossible-to-manage brat." Not only were his parents concerned, but his teacher had informed them that unless they got help for Gordie she would not allow him to continue in her class. As teachers themselves, Mr. and Mrs. Welles understood how difficult it is to control a class of twenty-six five-year-olds when just one of the students is disruptive, demanding, and provocative. What they could not understand was what had made Gordie change so.

I took the usual history. Pregnancy planned and uneventful. Birth full-term, no complications, perfect score on Apgar test (to evaluate the newborn's overall health and vigor). No problems eating or sleeping. All developmental landmarks average or slightly above average. Other than a mild case of chicken pox a year and a half earlier, Gordie had had no illnesses or hospitalizations, no major separation losses or family moves. He "adored" nursery school, learned well, and was popular. Both parents impressed me as caring, mature, thoughtful adults. They described their marriage as excellent until four months ago. That was when Gordie began to change and they began arguing about how to handle him. I was puzzled. Behavior changes do not pop out of nowhere. I continued to question. "When did you say Gordie's behavior changed?"

"Four months ago."

"Perhaps you could tell me what was happening four months ago—anything new, any change of any kind?"

June Welles nodded. "Donna was born four months ago, but Gordie was well prepared for her birth, he couldn't wait for the baby to come, and he adores her—so that can't be it. He hasn't shown any jealousy at all. He doesn't even get impatient with how long her feedings take, he just brings his blocks and crayons in to where we are and plays and talks to me and sings to her. They get along beautifully."

Clark Welles vigorously agreed. "We thought we'd have all that normal sibling-rivalry stuff, but we haven't. Gordie didn't even have a chance to miss his mother. She was only in the hospital four days and he went to see her every day. She even had time alone with Gordie when she came home, because Donna didn't leave the hospital for another week."

I pulled up my chair. "Why was that?" I asked.

They looked at, then away from each other. Mr. Welles began rubbing his jaw and clearing his throat. Mrs. Welles covered her face with her hands, then threw her head back and began a staccato, high-pitched report. "Donna was born with a cleft lip and cleft palate. Since she was full-term and a big baby they did surgery on her lip when she was only three days old. By the time she came home you could barely see the scar. They wanted me to bring her home on the sixth day, but I didn't want Gordie to be frightened by how hideous she looked so I insisted they keep her there until the stitches were out and the scar looked better. He doesn't know anything about it. You can't see the cleft palate unless you look into her mouth. They can't do anything about that until she's a year old and that'll be plenty of time to tell Gordie about it. That's a long way off. I'm worried about now. He doesn't know about Donna, he's asked no questions about her, and he gets along beautifully with her, so I don't think she has anything to do with his problems.''

And I was sure that she *did*. As I was sure that his parents' concern, disappointment, horror, and sadness (as well as other feelings I could only speculate about) had leaked out and were terrifying Gordie. Being frightened, Gordie, like all animal life, had two immediate options: he could fight or he could flee. I was heartened that Gordie had chosen to fight, for if he had fled into depression and withdrawal he would have been considerably more difficult to reach and to help. "What a terribly painful and difficult four months it must have been for you both," I said. "How hard you have both worked to give Donna the attention and care she needs and, at the same time, to protect Gordie from what you believe would frighten him. And with all the time and energy you've expended for your children, what's been left over to help you deal with your *own* feelings, individually and together?''

June Welles shook her head. "There hasn't been time enough to deal with all we have to *do,* much less with what we feel.''

"Perhaps, then, in an unexpected way, it's fortunate Gordie has been acting up. Now we can take the opportunity to look at the problems and worries you are all facing and find less painful ways of coping with them.''

As Clark Welles took his wife's hand she burst into

tears and quickly withdrew. Grabbing a tissue, she started apologizing, "I'm sorry, I'm sorry. I didn't mean to break down. I'm just so tired and worried, and now all of this. I don't dare cry in front of Gordie, so all Clark sees when we're alone is me crying. I never used to be like this." She averted her face from her husband. "You must hate me. First I give you a deformed baby, then I can't handle your son, and then I fall apart. I'm a failure as a mother, I'm a failure as a wife. I can't stand the idea of looking at a room of beautiful children, so I'm a failure as a teacher. Why don't you just get out while you still can!"

"Stop it! Just stop it!" Mr. Welles shouted, tears streaming down his face. "Damn it, what's the matter with you? You're the one with a degree in biology. I'm just a history teacher and even I know Donna's problem isn't your fault or mine. Don't you remember what the doctor said? No one in either of our families ever had Donna's problem. We couldn't have expected it, we couldn't have done anything about it! I can't stand it when you act like this. Do you realize how you've been pushing me away? You're smiling and loving with the kids, but with me you're either crying or angry. No, even that's not true, you've been coming down awfully hard on Gordie too, whenever he doesn't listen the first time or when he's mischievous. He's *never* listened the first time, he's always gotten into little-kid trouble. It never used to get you so upset. I see what's happening to you and then *I* start yelling at him. Poor kid, he's getting it from all sides."

"It seems you are all getting it from all sides," I said. "If we could explore together what appears to be happening to Gordie, it might give us some insight into what's hurting you."

Mr. Welles started us off by stressing how Gordie had changed over the last few months, from "a healthy, happy five-year-old."

"Five-year-olds almost always have mixed feelings about new siblings," I pointed out. "Yes, they feel happy and excited, but they also feel jealous and resentful about a new baby moving in on *their* territory. And then, if only subconsciously, they can believe that these feelings, wishes, and fears are powerful enough to make things happen. When Donna didn't come home from the hospital and you felt anxious and depressed, Gordie imagined that *he* was responsible for the baby's nonappearance and your being upset. Let's look at all the unexpected events that confronted Gordie suddenly. His sister did not come home when she was expected, his mother returned preoccupied and worried about the baby still in the hospital, she could not attend to him as he'd expected she would, and when Donna finally came home she looked different from the pictures of newborns he had seen. She also needed much more attention and time than he had expected."

Mrs. Welles said, "So Gordie was overloaded with surprises, and none of them good."

We reviewed how Gordie had been exposed to overhearing many conversations in the past few months. The Welleses acknowledged that he had often stood behind the door when they were on the phone, and would sometimes creep out of his bed at night and stand in the hallway listening to his parents talk. "He must have heard things he could only partly understand," I said, "things he distorted magically as many young children would. In direct conversation with Gordie, however, you've both told me he 'doesn't listen.' Perhaps that's because he's afraid of hearing more. He's been frightened by the bits and pieces he's overheard and assumed were his fault."

We explored the probability that Gordie's anger and defiance at home and school were ways of testing out whether he was still loved, a test he had made all the harder by the "badness" of his behavior. We wondered if it could also have been his way of getting punished for his "bad thoughts"—punishment being, after all, a very specific form of attention. And then, having succeeded in getting himself kicked out of school, a school he loved, he could well have found himself afraid that his parents would kick him out too.

Mr. Welles was shocked at the idea. "He couldn't think that! He knows we love him."

"That isn't the point," I said. "It's not what he knows that is giving him trouble, it's what he doesn't know. For example, five-year-olds still have fears that their bodies won't work well or reliably. Gordie sees Donna's physical problems as proof bodies don't work well. If it happened to her it could happen to him—he could even catch it from her. He already knows more than you wanted him to. The problem is he doesn't *understand* what he knows, what he hears, sees, and feels."

Mr. Welles said, "But we know Donna will be fine. The corrective surgery will repair her palate and . . ."

I was shaking my head. "Gordie doesn't understand any of that. And he can't on his own, with his powers of understanding still more magical than rational. So we have to help him, and the first thing we can do is give him a clear explanation of all that's happened and will happen. Then he won't be so terrified by his fantasies."

June Welles nodded. "I can understand everything you said about Gordie. I don't like it, but I understand and agree. We were trying to protect him, but, you're right, he must have felt the change in our attitude, and he must be aware that something is wrong with Donna's mouth. Like when he asked me why the nipple on Donna's bottle was so 'funny' . . . and I just sloughed it off and said there were lots of different kinds of nipples and bottles and I picked that one. But I'm confused about one thing. You said understanding Gordie would help give us insight into our own problems. Are you saying *we're* acting like five-year-olds?"

"Not at all. I'm saying all parents, no matter how adult or educated, feel guilty and responsible when their babies aren't perfect. We all regress under such stress to feeling we could have, or should have been able to prevent our baby's handicap. With some congenital handicaps that's true, but it certainly isn't true in the case of cleft lip and palate. And because we feel guilty and responsible we find ways to punish ourselves and deprive ourselves of the gratification and pleasure still available to us."

"And that would account for my irritability with Gordie and our arguments?" Mrs. Welles asked.

I nodded.

Clark Welles turned to his wife. "Honey, maybe we feel it's okay to get mad at Gordie just because he is so strong and healthy. As if we know we can argue with him and it'll work out. Sometimes when Donna is crying I wish she'd never been born and then I feel so ashamed—she's so little and helpless and has so much to go through. I don't dare direct my anger or disappointment to her so I get mad at you or Gordie. I guess I haven't been very helpful to you either."

With this session, situational crisis intervention was begun, four months later than I would have wished but still in time for the Welles family to pull together. I saw them for only six sessions before putting them on follow-up. Their success again pointed up that the better-functioning the family is before the stress, the more healthily and adaptively it will function through it. With June and Clark Welles's history of essentially excellent parenting, they needed only brief counseling to help Gordie give up his provocative behavior and regain his sense of security and self-assurance. Historically well nurtured and loved, Gordie was readily accessible to our efforts. Donna, despite her handicap, was an attractive, alert, and responsive infant. When she was ready for her palate surgery at thirteen months, Gordie and his parents were also prepared. This time Mrs. Welles remained in the hospital with Donna and Mr. Welles took personal leave from his job to remain with Gordie. Every day he took Gordie to see his sister and mother in the hospital. A second palate surgery was performed one year later, and soon afterward we had our final session. I smiled through it all as they told me how prepared they had been. I was no longer needed. They had one another again.

The Welles family had two major advantages over many other families of congenitally handicapped children. The handicap itself, cleft lip and palate, was curable. With surgery, speech training, and loving support, it was likely not only to be overcome, but even to disappear. The Welleses' second advantage was that neither they nor their physicians could have predicted her deformity; thus their guilt was not realistic. It was understandable and expectable, but it had no basis in fact.

The sad truth is that many thousands of babies are born with handicaps *that are predictable*. We can now identify many situations in which pregnant women carry a high risk of delivering a handicapped child: exposure to German measles in the first three months of pregnancy; exposure to radiation, multiple X ray, toxic substances such as high levels of mercury, and many drugs; syphilis; extremes of age (under eighteen or over forty). These are but a few of the physical conditions that raise the risk of producing a damaged child. Families with histories of diabetes, Tay-Sachs disease, sickle-cell anemia, Huntington's disease, again to mention but a few, are also at high risk.

Genetic counseling is available to all couples who wish to or are about to have a baby. Such counseling does not attempt to tell couples what they should or should not do; it concentrates on informing potential parents of the probability of giving birth to a handicapped baby. Some tests are sophisticated enough to diagnose a defect in an embryo in the first trimester of pregnancy (for example, amniocentesis can diagnose Down's syndrome). As a dedicated believer in primary prevention, I wish every couple that might be at risk would take advantage of genetic counseling. Parents should know what they face, and what it would mean to take on responsibility for a handicapped child. Some parents are able to nurture and love a handicapped child, to help it reach for and achieve everything available to it. Many others are not.

There should be no mistaking or underestimating the agonizing burden placed on parents who give birth to babies severely damaged, either mentally or physically—babies whose lives depend on artificial life-support systems, heroic measures that will in all probability be necessary for as long as they live; babies who despite the finest physical care will never be aware of or able to enjoy even the most primitive gratification of eating, locomotion, or recognition of parent or caretaker. I have to wonder at the "loving kindness" of those who demand such heroic measures. I do not intend to argue against the "right to life," but I do argue against, and even am suspicious of, those who demand the right to an artificial, mindless existence *for another human being*.

Teresa Patterson was referred to me shortly after contracting German measles in her second month of pregnancy. She had caught it from her husband, Brian, and their seven-year-old son, Darrell, both of whom had come down with the usually mild illness on a cub-scout overnight trip. Complaining of fever, malaise, and tenderness of the lymph nodes around her ears, Mrs. Patterson consulted her family doctor, who immediately referred her to her obstetrician. Dr. Andrea Lynd examined her and diagnosed rubella. Teresa Patterson was not alarmed; she felt achy and uncomfortable, but not very sick. Dr. Lynd explained that Mrs. Patterson would be fine in a few days and would probably experience no side effects herself, but the baby she was carrying was now at high risk of being born with cataracts, heart defects, deafness, and profound mental retardation. Compassionately and firmly, she recommended a therapeutic abortion. Teresa Patterson refused absolutely. She could not believe such a mild illness could so devastatingly affect her unborn child. **Dr. Lynd** asked to speak to her husband. Brian Patterson was stunned but also disbelieving. He listened to **Dr. Lynd's** explanation that the baby had a 25 percent chance of being born with encephalitis, glaucoma, bone marrow disease, and severe growth problems. When the Pattersons still agreed that they would take their chances, Dr. Lynd referred them to me, hoping I could help them explore their decision though without necessarily trying to change their minds. Most of all, the pediatrician was concerned about the "guilt trip" their son Darrell would be on if the baby were to be born handicapped. Despite the double referral, the Pattersons would not come—until six months later when their baby was born prematurely: blind, deaf, microcephalic, and profoundly retarded.

I have no way of knowing if the Pattersons *could* have explored their decision with me, or if I would have been able to prepare them better for the tragedy of their baby's birth. They came to see me only once, ostensibly to get help for Darrell, who as Dr. Lynd had predicted was as consumed with guilt as were his parents. I tried, how I tried, to help them realize they *did* have realistic reasons for feeling guilty, but because they had erred with one child didn't mean they had to err with Darrell or each other. I explained that while there was little they could do to help their baby, there was a great deal they could do to help Darrell. He blamed himself for catching German measles, for giving the illness to his mother, and for deforming the baby. Since none of these was his fault, they could ease his mind with regard to them as unrealistic guilts. And they could also, I hoped aloud, convince him that their decision not to terminate the pregnancy came from wishing, waiting, and not believing what they could not see, rather than out of hatred or lack of caring. They agreed to bring Darrell to see me three days later, but failed to show up for the appointment. I called the Patterson home, but there was no answer. I called the hospital where the baby was in intensive care, only to be told the baby had died hours before. I felt both saddened and relieved. The baby hadn't had a chance for life. I continued calling the Pattersons until their phone was disconnected. Two days later I read in the paper that Mr. Patterson had been killed instantly when his car "went out of control" and crashed into an abutment. I wrote to Mrs. Patterson, but my letter was returned, "Addressee moved; no forwarding address." One family—two people dead, two running in terrorized desperation. Then I cried. It helped me a little, them not at all.

As mentioned earlier in this chapter, acquired handicaps pose a different set of problems from congenital handicaps. Being accustomed to unimpeded, voluntary, and reliable body functioning, those who acquire handicaps suffer not only the limitations set upon their physical or mental functioning, but also an acute and prolonged sense of loss for the body part or body function. Our sense of self-esteem is after all related to our ability to meet expectations, and when an arm, leg, eye, or part of the brain can no longer perform, we are not only frustrated, we are also in mourning for the loss of that part of ourselves. Our reaction becomes narcissistic, and is further compounded by our being subjected to the pitying or avoiding responses of family, friends, and strangers, which only make us feel even more helpless and disgusting. It is a vicious cycle, but not a necessary one.

Dr. Sam Mazell called me late one afternoon. A specialist in rehabilitation medicine, he could growl like a grizzly bear or be as gentle as a kitten. Today he just sounded tired. "Ann, if you've got a minute I'd like to talk to you about a kid I just saw, a seventeen-year-old boy whose leg was blown off in a gas explosion yesterday morning. I was with him and his parents when he woke up a while ago. It was pretty grim.''

He told me about it, how Rod Steele awakened from his coma complaining of a severe headache, crushing pressure on his chest, and agonizing pain in his right leg. When Sam asked him what he remembered, Rod could recall only entering the office building with his delivery, a huge blast, and being tossed through the air—then nothing. Rod's parents, Terry and Erica Steele, were crying as Sam explained to Rod that he'd been half buried under the debris. ''I told him his headache was due to a bad concussion, that he had sustained five broken ribs, and the pressure was from the tight bandages we had to apply. He interrupted me and said his leg hurt so badly, and he wanted to know if it was broken or just bruised. I had to tell him, Ann. I told him his leg was so badly torn and crushed that we couldn't save it, we tried but we couldn't. I told him we had to amputate below the knee. He just looked at me and then he screamed. Jesus! I'll never forget it. He screamed, *'No! No!* You're *lying!* It couldn't hurt so if you amputated it. Why are you lying to me!' And then he kept moving his left leg trying to find his right leg. He couldn't, and he became very still. And he whispered, 'It's gone. My leg is gone. You bastard! Why didn't you let me die?' That's when it hit the fan.''

Sam went on to tell me how Mrs. Steele started yelling at Rod to ''Stop it'' and Mr. Steele began rocking his son like a baby, telling him to yell, cry, telling him everything would be all right. ''Rod looked at us as if we were crazy. 'All right! What do you mean all right! A one-legged skier, a one-legged tennis player. All right! A *freak!* That's what I'll be, a *freak!*' That's when I blasted him, Ann. Hell, that kid doesn't know what a freak is. I told him he was talking pure bullshit. I told him he had every right to be scared and angry, but he didn't know what the hell he was talking about. You know what I mean. I let him know that we could fit him to an artificial leg, and that he'd have to work hard and learn to use it, and if he worked hard enough he would be able to ski again. I also told him he was in the best rehab unit in the city, and we don't waste our time. Then I ordered morphine for him to kill the pain and let him rest. He was worn out and so were his parents. I wasn't feeling so great myself.''

I told Sam that he might not be feeling great, but I thought he'd combined cussing and caring very effectively. Then I asked him what he wanted me to do. Sam's only concern about Rod's physical recovery and rehabilitation was that his morale might remain so low that he wouldn't fight his way through it. Sam asked me to see Rod and his parents to help them adapt constructively to Rod's handicap and lift Rod's morale. I agreed and told Sam to have the Steeles call me.

Interestingly, but not surprisingly, when the Steeles did come to consult me it was not about Rod, but out of concern for his thirteen-year-old brother, Chip. In the month since the explosion Chip had become highly irritable. More alarmingly, he had had two accidents in the past three weeks. The first occurred when he dropped his weight-lifting equipment on his right foot, breaking three toes. Two weeks later, visiting Rod in the hospital, Chip caught sight of his brother's stump. In horror he raced out of the room and, impeded by his broken toes, slipped and fell, this time suffering a fracture of his right leg.

Erica Steele was distraught. ''Chip never was accident-prone before. Quite the opposite. Ever since he was little he has been in training for one sport or another. I can understand Rod being depressed and angry, but I can't understand why Chip is so upset and suddenly so careless. It's almost as if he wants to get hurt.''

I agreed with Mrs. Steele. ''It *is* easier to understand

why Rod is having a difficult time, but strangely he's better able to cope with the loss of his leg. He has a huge support system around him: his parents, doctors, nurses, rehabilitation therapists, and other patients just as, or even more, handicapped than he is. He can actively work to master his disability. Chip is a survivor. He can't do anything active to help his brother or to make up his loss to him. Tell me, have Chip and Rod been equally competitive athletically?''

Mrs. Steele said they had, ''though Chip always chose different sports. He's on the track team and the soccer team at his junior high, and he's really good. He spends hours at practice and then he comes home and trains more with his weights. This year Rod started teaching him tennis. He told him that Chip would probably be beating him by the end of the season. Rod's always admired Chip's coordination, and Chip's known Rod thought he was good.''

''Still, I imagine there have been times when Chip was resentful and jealous of Rod's greater skills,'' I said, ''even just being his kid brother. Now, suddenly, Chip is the more skillful. Sure, it's a position he wanted to achieve, but not at the expense of Rod losing his leg. He feels guilty and helpless—and probably ashamed of how horrified or disgusted he was when he saw the mutilation. No one is punishing him for his previous jealousy or his current 'shameful behavior,' so he has to punish himself—he had to let himself get hurt.''

''But Chip's not a baby, he can't really believe he had anything to do with Rod's accident.''

''No, he's not a baby, but we never get too old to wonder, 'Why him? Why not me?' when someone we're very close to gets badly hurt and we survive. We never get too old to regret all the mean or nasty things we've said or felt about that person. You were right when you said Chip wants to get hurt, but he's not consciously aware of it. He's only aware of how miserable he feels. And Rod is likely to make him feel worse. Feeling so lousy and frustrated himself, he may well take it out on Chip. Until he's walking again—and maybe not even then. He'll resent his prosthesis and anyone who's physically intact.''

Erica Steele nodded. ''I think I know how Rod feels. I've been such a bitch. Every time Rod's friends come to visit, I resent them. I resent their walking free and unhurt while Roddy has to struggle so hard. I'm glad they come, I know it's good for Rod, but I still resent them. Don't you resent them too, Terry?''

''No,'' said her husband, ''I don't think I feel that way. I know what you mean, but I don't resent them. Maybe a little jealous, but not resentful.''

''Mr. and Mrs. Steele, you and your sons each have your own feelings and problems stimulated by Rod's injury. Now's the time for us all to get together to talk them out, so that it's no longer necessary to enact them. Does that make sense to you?''

It did. Two days later I met with the whole family in Rod's hospital room. As we entered Rod was shouting, ''Shit! Damn it, Mule, I *am* swinging!'' Mule, a boy of eight or nine, wearing thick orthopedic shoes, his lower body encased in leather and steel braces, was demonstrating his skill on crutches. ''Shit, Rod, you ain't even tryin'! You gotta learn to swing, man, swing! Put your crutches way in front, weight on your arms, and swing. Hell, my swing is twice as long as yours and I don't even come up to your belly button.''

We moved into the room and Mule caught sight of Chip with his leg in a cast. ''Wow, you too? Wanna join the practice?'' Chip glowered. ''Beat it, Mule! Who needs you!''

''Hey, cool it!'' Rod barked, dropping exhausted into a chair. ''Come back later, huh, Mule. We can go to P.T. [physical therapy] together. And pay no attention to Chip, he's just being his rotten self.''

Mule swung out of the room making a heavy thunking

sound each time his feet hit the floor. Rod turned on his brother, "Listen, Punk, you make another crack to Mule and I'll break your other leg! That kid's been like that all his life and he'll never walk without those braces and crutches. He's had six operations, and that's the best they can do for him. They said he'd never get out of a wheelchair, and look at him! He's got more guts than you and me put together. So just shut up!" He wiped the sweat off his face. "Hi, Mom, Dad." He turned to me. "You must be Ms. Kliman. Sorry you came in on all this."

"I'm not," I said, smiling. "In fact, I'm glad to see you so mad. Sounds like Mule's fighting spirit has rubbed off on you."

"You better believe it! I thought there was nothing worse than losing a leg. My God, he's got two legs and neither of them will ever work because his spine never grew right. He has to wear diapers like a baby, but he's tough as nails, and funny too. I've seen guys upstairs with flippers instead of arms, with no legs at all, one guy with half his face gone, and a kid who looks fine only he can't move or talk. They move his body for him. At first it made me sick to go up there, it made me want to throw up just to look at them. Then I realized it probably made them sick when they looked at my stump. It makes *me* sick to look at it. Was that a trip! And then I got mad. Really mad! Helpless, crippled, hell! They're people and they feel. Just like anyone else. That's when I met Mule, and that's when I decided I was still me. Leg or not, I'm still me. I get down, frustrated, mad, and tired. Really wiped out. Like this morning when they fitted me for the artificial leg. God, did that hurt. I swore and yelled, but they made me try it and when it was over my knee felt like it was on fire and I was so beat I couldn't even get into the wheelchair alone. But I did it, and I'll do it again. . . . Hmmmmmmmm, that was some speech. Sorry!"

Mrs. Steele gave Rod a quick kiss. "Honey, I'm so proud of you."

"Mom, don't say that! It makes me feel like an idiot."

"I didn't mean it that way, Rod, I only meant . . ." Her voice faltered.

I said, "Rod, maybe your mother needs to say what she's feeling just the way you needed to a moment ago. As do Chip and your dad. You all have choices now. You can have the courage to say what you feel no matter how pleasant or unpleasant, and you can exercise the choice of hearing what is said as a put-down or as that person's need to share."

"Okay, fair enough. Then I have the right to say that it makes me feel like an idiot when Mom says she's proud of me for learning something I should have known long ago."

"And I have the right to feel good about my son who has grown and learned more than many people do in a lifetime."

Chip sat quietly listening. I turned to him. "Chip, you really got blasted a few minutes ago. Since then Rod and your parents have been talking about how they feel. You haven't said a word about how you feel. And I'm sure you're feeling a lot. So rather than break another bone I suggest you break out of your shell and tell us what's tearing you apart."

He looked at Rod and then quickly, impulsively began to talk. "Rod, listen, I don't know how to say this without sounding either mean or crazy. But listen. When I found out what happened to you I got scared. Really scared. I mean, the idea of you being crippled for the rest of your life just about killed me. And all I could think of was all the times I bugged you 'cause you were the big shot, and I was glad you couldn't be the big shot anymore, only I just freaked." He burst into tears.

Mrs. Steele rose to go to him, but Rod grabbed her hand. "Let him cry, Mom. Now you listen, Punk. So you got scared, so you freaked. Big deal! But to break your toes and then your leg, that's dumb! You think it made me feel any better? Does it make you feel any better?"

"Yeeees!"

"Christ, I don't believe it! Chip, it makes you feel lousy! Look everybody, would you all get out of here for a while and let me and the punk talk . . . please?"

His parents and I went to the waiting room. Mr. Steele was telling his wife it was good for the boys to battle it out, but she was shaking. "It's not their battling that upsets me, it's me. After all these years of bringing up the boys and feeling pretty good about them and myself, suddenly I don't know how to react to them. Or rather when I do I only get them more upset. It's as if I lost my judgment when Rod lost his leg. Remember how I screamed at him when he said he wanted to die? I couldn't bear to hear him talk like that. And just now he was insulted when I said I was proud of him. I don't know *what* to say anymore. I feel so helpless."

Mr. Steele tried to assure his wife that she shouldn't "feel like that," but then I pointed out that what she was saying was in good part true—she *did* feel helpless that she couldn't take Rod's pain away, or make Chip less scared and angry. But then the boys felt helpless too, that was why they were so irritable with their parents and each other. But now Rod was no longer feeling so helpless, he was beginning to work actively on making himself less dependent on others. "Rod is even trying to share what he's achieved with Chip. He's not going to 'forgive' Chip, he's going to help Chip forgive himself—and, hopefully, like himself again. Perhaps that's what you need to do too."

It was. It took only a few sessions for Erica Steele to accept that there were several areas in which she realistically could not help or protect her sons. She began to find ways in which she could be supportive without infantilizing them, and simultaneously she began to feel less threatened by the anger they displaced onto her. As she felt more comfortable with her sons' growing ability to do for themselves, her self-esteem rose and her concern about her judgment abated. Chip was greatly reassured by Rod's determination and success in mastering his artificial leg. In fact, by the end of six months, Rod was again the "big shot" and Chip could complain about it again—but now safely.

So far I have been discussing people whose handicaps, whether congenital or acquired, are readily observable. There are, however, millions of people whose handicaps, even though severe, are not obvious. Because these people *seem* to be unimpaired, their abnormal behavior is frequently the butt of ridicule or outrage. It's almost as if the general population were saying, "How dare you fool me!" Think of how often you have heard someone yell at a pedestrian who crosses against the light, "What's the matter with you, you blind?!"—blind being used as a curse word. Our speech is sprinkled with statements referring to sensory or intellectual handicaps as expressions of hostility and anger. We speak and act as if the people afflicted with blindness, deafness, or retardation *intended* to insult us, or at least endanger us.

Lynne Draper was subjected to such treatment when, at age eleven, she became blind following a case of encephalitis. An only child whose parents worked full-time, Lynne was dependent on school friends and neighbors for daytime social contact. Prior to her illness she had enjoyed great popularity; she had a highly developed sense of humor and was a remarkably skilled guitarist. However, when she developed encephalitis and was hospitalized, friends and neighbors rarely visited. Nor did they write or send flowers or toys. When Lynne returned home, now totally blind but otherwise healthy, her isolation continued. Neighbors didn't drop in, friends didn't call; and to intensify her sense of loss, Lynne had to transfer to a school for the blind. In the space of a few weeks she had lost her sight, her friends, her school. Mr. and Mrs. Draper tried desperately to reestablish Lynne's world. They spent hours calling the mothers of Lynne's friends, trying to set up sleep-overs, supper invitations,

Saturday skating parties, Sunday concerts—anything so Lynne could have contact with friends again. But there were always excuses.

The harder they tried, the quicker and harsher the refusals became. Lynne stopped trying—she seemed to know she had become a pariah. Unlike Rod Steele whose sudden handicap mobilized a masterful energy, Lynne succumbed passively to a sightless, friendless world. At her new school she appeared unresponsive to the overtures made by classmates. They began to consider her "stuck-up," and she became the butt of teasing. She did her work, but no more. Because her work tended to be very good, even with the little energy she invested in it, her teachers expressed no concern about her intellectual progress. They were, however, concerned about her listless and slow learning of Braille. They felt she "just isn't trying." And while assuring the Drapers that it wasn't unusual for newly blind children to be resistant to Braille, they recommended psychological intervention to "get her over the hump."

Vince and Belle Draper were convinced that the trouble lay with Lynne's friends, not Lynne. "They're the ones who are acting crazy." They renewed their campaign to get Lynne and her old friends together. It was the mother of Lynne's "best friend" who finally came right out with it. "Look, Belle, I don't want to seem cruel or unfeeling, but it's just not fair of you to expect Edie to want to play with Lynne. After all, it would be a strain on Edie, she'd have to take care of Lynne, not play with her. I think it's just too depressing a situation to put my child in. And it's not fair to Lynne to expect her to play with normal children. After all, we all do best with our own kind." Belle Draper slammed the telephone down so hard she smashed the mouthpiece. She then went into her bedroom, shut the door, and wept. And she called me.

In my first session with Mr. and Mrs. Draper I just

listened at the start. Like their daughter, they too had been shunned and avoided. They needed to talk. They spoke of the days of terrified waiting, not knowing if Lynne would live or die—and then the horror of hearing she would be blind. Vince Draper confessed he almost wished Lynne had died. "At least then she wouldn't have had to face a lifetime of helplessness in a world without friends." His wife said they had spent half the night crying when they got the news, and the rest of the night planning. "We were determined Lynne would get the best possible care and treatment. We were determined that she not become an object of pity. We never thought she would be treated like a leper. We thought if she learned to live with her blindness, if she learned Braille, went to school, eventually got a guide dog, she could have a full life. We were determined to help her in every way possible. What we didn't anticipate was how much *we* would have to learn and relearn. It was a shock to realize Lynne was like a baby again. She can't feed or dress herself, she can't bathe herself without help, she can't move about the house without the risk of hurting herself. She has to be watched constantly. And by now she's so withdrawn she *won't* learn, even what she can. She won't practice what they teach her at school. She just sits in her darkness. She won't even listen to the music she used to love. Her favorite was Stevie Wonder; how's that for irony! Instead of being reassured and inspired by his example, she just covers her ears. We don't know what to do for her anymore. Lynne has lost her sight, but it feels like we've lost our child."

I told them I thought I understood. "In becoming blind Lynne has not only lost her sight, she's lost the sense of herself. Her withdrawal and passivity are signs of how profoundly she feels her inner and outer world have changed. So it's no wonder you both feel she has become alien to you. She has. While there may be little we can do to make her old friends return, there may be a great deal we can do to facilitate *her* return. I say facilitate because it may be that too much is being done *for* Lynne. Because she feels helpless about feeding or dressing herself doesn't mean we have to accept her helplessness. She may need to be done *with*, but not done *for*." I pointed out how, since she had no control over her blindness, it was all the more crucial that she exercise control over as much else as she could. To baby her was no way to help her regain her self-esteem and self-confidence. "The more competent she becomes, the better she will feel. And the less sorry she feels for herself, the less sorry people are likely to feel for her. She needs to have reasonable demands made on her, she needs to develop reasonable expectations for herself. That will only come with support, firmness, and caring, from you and the school."

"But she's not *able* to help herself yet."

"Mr. Draper, she has to be able to help herself. At first she may be clumsy, messy, and unsure, but she needs to start being responsible for herself. The longer she is expected to be helpless, the longer she will be helpless."

Mrs. Draper turned to her husband. "Vince, do you remember when I had my appendix out? Remember how I thought I'd have to be in bed for a week, and how depressed and rotten I felt. When they came in six hours after surgery and told me to get up and walk, I told them I couldn't, I hurt too much and felt too weak. But they made me, and once I was up and moving I felt so much better. Maybe, in a much bigger way, it's the same for Lynne. It wouldn't be so terrible if she buttoned her clothes wrong, or spilled her juice—or even fell occasionally. At least she'd be up and moving."

"Honey, I have no trouble with that. We'll just have to find a way to explain to Lynne what we're doing. But then how do you say to a kid, I'm pushing you and not helping you because I love you?"

"But we *will* be helping her . . . to help herself. And we've got to convince ourselves of that before we can convince Lynne."

Of course they were right. I met several more times with the Drapers, and before meeting with Lynne I consulted with her school to learn just how they were going to teach Lynne to be self-sufficient, so that we could work in concert and be an integrated support system for Lynne and her parents. I also thought a great deal about what it's like to be blind. In college I had a close friend who'd been blind since birth. We were helpful to each other. I used to read to her for an hour each day, and she helped me learn (and pass with honors) a course in statistics—a course I had been sure I would fail. Having lived with, worked with, and enjoyed my year with Helena, I was convinced blind people do not have to be helpless, friendless, or miserable.

When I met Lynne for the first time three weeks later she wasn't at all withdrawn or passive. She was furious. When I asked her what she understood about coming to see me, she retorted, "Because I'm blind! What's the matter with you, are *you* blind, or just stupid!"

"I know you're blind, Lynne, that's something terrible that's happened to you, but what else are you besides blind?"

"What do you mean, 'what else?'? I'm blind. Don't you understand? You're just like my parents! When I knock something over or fall, they don't say a word. They act as if they don't know. Why won't they help me? They just don't care anymore. They probably wish I were dead. I do too."

"Lynne, you're telling me you think being blind and being stupid is the same. You're saying being blind is like being dead. If your mother had encephalitis and were blinded, would you think she was stupid, would you wish her dead?"

"No, but I'd help her! I'd help her all the time. I wouldn't make her feel even worse by telling her to do something she couldn't."

"Before you were blinded did you like your mother to baby you? You had eleven years to care for yourself. You had all that time to know yourself and your world. Now suddenly you can't see your world, and you can't see yourself as you used to. What you're actually telling me is that because you can't use your eyes anymore you aren't you anymore."

There was a long silence before Lynne said, "What do you look like?"

"Do you want me to tell you what I look like, or would you like to know for yourself?"

"That's mean! How could I know for myself when I can't see you?"

"Blind people learn to read words with their fingers. They can also 'read' people with their fingers . . . and their ears. If we stand next to each other you can tell how tall I am by listening to where my voice is coming from. You can tell what my face is like by feeling it with your fingers. Would you like to find out for yourself what I look like? And what you can't find out by touching I'll try to tell you."

Lynne hesitated, then stood up and asked me to stand beside her. I let her know when I was close to her, on her left side, and told her to find out what she could about me. She put her hand flat on her head, then moved it straight out toward me. She touched my shoulder, moved her hand up my neck, then over my face and through my hair. She began to giggle. "You're tall, and you wear glasses, and your nose has a bump at the end. Your hair is long, and you're skinny."

I laughed. "You certainly found out a lot about me."

"But I don't know what color your hair or eyes or skin are."

"No, that you can't tell by touch. My hair is dark brown, my eyes are hazel, and my skin is quite tanned. But what else can you 'read' about me?"

"Your voice is very soft and you're wearing a sweater and a pin."

"Right! Describe the pin to me."

Lynne took her time until her fingertips had traced

enough of the pin for her to describe its shape, composition, and texture. She smiled when I again complimented her on her accuracy. "And do you think you'd have had as good a picture of me if I had just told you what I look like?" I put to her.

"Well, I'd have understood what you said, but I wouldn't know it for myself."

"Exactly. And isn't it a more comfortable feeling to know for yourself?"

"But there's so *much* to know! I get scared."

"Of course you do, that's why you need people to help you help yourself. But if they do everything for you you'll never know for yourself. And it can be awfully hard for grown-ups to let children help themselves, even when kids are not blind. And it's especially hard for your parents."

Lynne nodded. "I know Mommy and Daddy love me, but my friends . . . they don't seem to anymore. They won't come over and visit, and they never call."

"Lynne, you said it's scary being blind. I bet it's scary for your friends too. Maybe as you discover that you are still yourself, even though you're blind, you'll be less scared. The more you can be at ease with yourself, the more your friends will be able to be at ease with you. It's worth a try, don't you agree?"

"I don't know. I want to, but I get scared and mad and sometimes I just don't want to do anything . . . like when I came in here I didn't want to talk to you. I didn't even want to come at all." Lynne gave me a quick little smile. "But I'll come back if you want me to." I told her I did, very much, and we made her next appointment.

Over the next six months we worked often and well together. And we always worked hard. Never a particularly neat or organized child, Lynne had to reorient herself to maintaining a state of order, so she could know reliably her position in relation to the objects around her. Her teachers and parents were invaluable in preserving such a structure, as well as in teaching her tricks and guidelines to "see" without eyes. To me she expressed her irritation with the precision she had to develop, her impatience, anger, and frustration, and her sadness and yearning. She spoke poignantly of the things she would never see again: the elaborately designed quilt on her bed, a sunrise, a Christmas tree being lit, movies, the exhibits at the Museum of Natural History, a full moon, flowers. She wept when she thought of all she would never see: the Grand Canyon, Disney World, her own children. As she was able to express these feelings more and more freely, Lynne became less and less fearful. She began investing her time and energy in learning to live with and master her disability. She was surprised how rapidly and easily some things came. It took her little time to maneuver skillfully in her own home and to be responsible for her personal care. Braille remained difficult until she returned to her guitar. As she rediscovered the joy in feeling the strings and making music, she discovered the joy of feeling letters and reading with her fingers. She laughed with me about having to take care not to overdo the guitar " 'cause I'll get calluses on my fingertips and then I won't be able to read!''

Just as important as the development of new compensatory skills was Lynne's new way of relating to people. As her competence and self-assurance increased, she began reaching out to people. At first she confined her overtures to children at her school, children who would understand her limitations. She was able to explain that she really wasn't "stuck-up"— just scared. The kids responded with their own stories and soon she had two "good friends" and lots of "friendly friends." Cheered by her success she began to engage herself with the sighted world. She handled misguided pity matter-of-factly, "Yeah, being blind stinks!" and cloying pity scornfully, "You trying to get a merit badge?" In response to the continued rejection of several of her old friends, Lynne wrote a song entitled, "Losing Sight of What Really Counts," a clever, ironic ditty about those who were blinder than she.

After she sang and played her song for me we decided our work was just about finished. I still see Lynne on follow-up. Now a young adolescent with all the developmental difficulties and hassles of any teenager, she is growing, learning, and living well—even exuberantly. When I see her parents they worry and complain, not about Lynne's blindness but because she stays up too late, forgets to do her chores, doesn't listen as she used to—they worry and complain as do all parents of healthy adolescents. They also delight in her humor, warmth, and accomplishments.

Patients
and Hospitals

4

Less than a century ago a hospital was a place where one went to die. The state of medicine was still terribly primitive, lacking anything like the knowledge and technology we now take for granted—the antibiotics and vaccines, electrocardiographs, safe, stable anesthesia, reliable laboratory tests, surgical techniques, and instruments advanced far beyond those of the old-time "barber surgeons." The spirit of nursing care may have been epitomized by a Clara Barton or a Florence Nightingale, but usually there was little an experienced nurse could do other than bathe the fevered and offer a soothing word. Often the hospital building was dark, odoriferous, and grim. And the physicians themselves were a breed apart. They knew all that could be known, little enough in those days, and they were not to be questioned. Aloof and remote from the patient and his family, they kept their own counsel on matters of life and death. No wonder fear and helplessness were the common lot of the hospitalized.

With modern advances of medical and surgical technology, the vast majority of hospitalized patients today do not die. The means and ability to cure and to treat have come further in the past forty years than in all the preceding centuries. Hospitals have been made more pleasant, with such features as brightly painted walls and nonglare lighting. Now we enter hospitals with the hope of living.

For too many of us, however, the experience is still accompanied by fear and a sense of helplessness. It is an irony of modern life that the more scientifically sophisticated our hospitals have become, the less do they minister to the patient. The more nurses are trained to perform such critical tasks as monitoring machines, checking IVs, suctioning, and administering medication, the less time they have to comfort the patient. And physicians, remote once by virtue of their station, are remote today within the bounds of specialization and bureaucracy. Such apparent callousness is not, I believe, the intent or wish of medical professionals. They too suffer as hidden victims.

There has been a reaction, a growing concern about the dehumanization of hospital patients. A countermovement for "humanistic medicine" is slowly gaining popularity. As one of its effects, many excellent hospitals have radically changed their visiting hours, recognizing that family and friends can as likely accelerate healing as impede it, even for the critically ill, and particularly for children. Some hospitals have gone so far as to provide daybeds for parents of hospitalized children, or for the spouse of an adult parent. Some hospitals offer a "Patient's Bill of Rights" to each admission and have a "Patient Representative" available to answer questions and act as advocate. Regrettably, the hospitals participating in such practices are still few.

Illness and pain can make the strongest of us regress to a more dependent state. When compounded by anxiety, such dependency can erode our psychic resources to a point of helplessness, even hopelessness. We become vulnerable to "giving up," to responding more poorly to treatment, even to developing secondary complications.

Our reactions to being hospitalized depend, of course,

on the kind of hospitalization we must undergo. Prolonged hospitalization is usually a draining experience for both patients and their families. Hospitalization for diagnostic purposes excites anxiety; since neither we nor our physicians know what is wrong, we tend to imagine the worst. Sudden, unexpected hospitalization interferes with our psychological balance and sense of security. Hospitalization requiring some mutilating surgery assaults not only our bodies but our sense of the body's intactness and inviolability. And hospitalization of young children, for whatever reason, provokes anxieties of separation, and thrusts the children into strange surroundings and new authorities—people who give orders not only to the children but to their parents. For very young children, too immature to be comfortable with their outer appearance, much less with what is inside them, there can be a special fear of all procedures that cause pain or take away any part of them—even parts for which they have yet no name or clear awareness.

Barry Price was five and a half when he was referred to us by his pediatrician prior to surgical repair of a hernia. Fran Price, Barry's mother, told me, "He's a very healthy little boy. I just don't want this to be a traumatic experience for him, and Dr. Hames told me you prepare children for surgery. Barry's never even seen a hospital so he has no idea what to expect."

"We do help prepare children for surgery," I told Mrs. Price, "and we've learned that the fewer surprises they are exposed to, the easier it is for them to adapt. Let me get in touch with the surgeon so I can find out precisely what to expect. I'll also call the hospital and arrange for a prehospitalization visit for Barry so the place will not be strange to him."

Mrs. Price agreed and we briefly discussed how she would tell Barry about coming to see me. I suggested, "It would be helpful if you told Barry that while this is a place to visit and play, we also *work* here to help children with their ideas and worries about having an operation."

The next day Barry walked into my office with his mother—or rather strode in. He was a sturdy, stocky boy who greeted me with a wide grin. He looked carefully around the room. "Wow, you sure got a lot of stuff here! Can I play with the blocks?" I told him he could, and within minutes he had constructed a tall building as sturdy as he was. While he was demonstrating his considerable architectural skill I was asking him what he understood about coming to see me. Keeping his attention on the blocks, he told me, "Mommy said it's about the operation to fix my bump. Only I've had it a long time and I don't know why they have to fix it now." Adding still more blocks to the already tall building, he continued, "It's a *big* bump. I can poke it and it goes back inside, but it always pops out again." He looked up at me and grinned.

I smiled. "It sounds like you are proud of that bump, Barry. Maybe you're not so sure you want the doctors to fix it."

As Barry turned to face me his elbow grazed a block and the top part of his building fell down. He started and immediately grabbed his genitals. I said, "When the top of your building fell off you really looked scared. I know you're not afraid of the blocks, so maybe you're trying to tell me you have some scary ideas about your bump and what's going to happen to it."

Barry turned away from the building and began playing with some small cars. He was shaking his head. "I *like* my bump. Why do they have to take it off?"

Mrs. Price said, "Honey, they're not going to take your bump off. They're going to tuck it back in where it belongs and then sew up the hole in the muscle."

I added, "It's necessary so it doesn't get pinched and

become painful. Also, the operation will make you as strong as other children and keep you out of danger.''

Barry was scrunched up, holding himself tightly. "But Mommy, you told me when they do the operation they would cut me. All my blood will run out! And when I'm all bloody how will they see what to sew . . . maybe they'll sew up the wrong thing!''

I said, "Barry, that's a very, very scary thought. Lots of children your age have worries that doctors may sew up the wrong thing, or take off the wrong thing. Lots of kids worry that they might lose something very important, like all their blood. Maybe you have some other scary ideas which you could tell me.''

Barry stood up and moved closer to his mother. "It's gonna hurt a lot. You told me, Mommy, they'd put me to sleep, but things hurt when you sleep. Remember when I got sick and my tummy hurt so much I woke up and threw up right in my bed?''

Realizing that Barry didn't understand the difference between sleep and anesthesia, I explained that people can feel pain when they are asleep, but emphasized that he would not be asleep during the operation. I told him the doctor would give him a special medication called anesthesia which would make him unconscious for the whole time the doctors would be fixing his bump. I further explained that when someone is unconscious he cannot wake up or feel pain until all the medicine is used up, and added that one doctor would be with him during the entire surgery and his only job would be to make sure that Barry was getting all the anesthesia he needed. "Maybe if I can tell you exactly what is going to happen you won't be scared. You still won't like being in the hospital or having the operation, but you won't have to be scared either.'' Barry told me to go ahead.

For the next fifteen minutes I drew pictures for Barry showing him what a hernia is, what his bump was, and explained what would happen to him from the moment he checked into the hospital. I told him about the needle prick in his finger for blood tests and agreed it would hurt for a second. I also assured him that all his blood wouldn't run out, either with the needle prick or the operation. I told him the nurses would want him to make pee-pee in a bottle and he said that was silly. I explained the blood and urine samples would tell the doctors a lot about how his body was working, and the more they knew about him the more they could help him. I told him that while children aren't so sure of what's inside them, doctors know very well, and I assured him that his surgeon wouldn't get mixed up.

We made a clay boy complete with hernia and genitals (I forgot the hair on his head, but Barry reminded me) and we did some pretend surgery. The clay boy came to after surgery and I explained how sort of dizzy and sleepy and confused the clay boy felt, and that's why he was in bed with high sides so he couldn't fall out. I told him the clay boy didn't feel very good *after* the operation and had some pain where the bandage was. The clay boy's mommy was there to comfort him, and the nurse gave him some medicine to take away the pain. We talked about how important it was for the clay boy to walk so his muscles wouldn't get cramped. The clay boy cried when he felt uncomfortable, but no one got angry because they knew how hard it is for a small boy to be in a hospital. The session ended with Barry agreeing to come back to see me two days later, the day he was to enter the hospital. Barry left carrying the drawings and the clay boy so he could tell his older sister "all about my operation."

Barry visited the hospital the next day. He saw the children's unit where he would be staying, met the nurses, and was taken to look at an operating room. When I saw him again he told me, "I like the playroom and the nurses, but the operation room is too shiny. It hurts my eyes." I reminded him that he would be unconscious when he was taken into that room and he wouldn't be able to feel any hurt. Barry then took out the clay boy and spent the rest of the session "operating," giving shots, and encouraging the clay boy to walk, "even if it hurts a little—it won't hurt too much, clay boy." At one point his "scalpel" slipped and the incision came dangerously close to the clay boy's penis. Barry gasped and quickly covered the incision with more clay—adding clay to the penis "just in case." I told him he was still a little boy who was only pretending to do surgery, and a real grown-up surgeon wouldn't make such a scary mistake. Barry looked at me condescendingly and said, "I know that!"

Barry weathered the hospitalization very well. His mother remained with him and encouraged him to be as active as possible and to talk about what he was feeling. His father visited him every morning and brought his sister to see him every evening. Barry complained appropriately, cooperated when necessary, and healed well. When I saw him on follow-up ten days later, he was marvelous! He had the clay boy with him and he showed me the stitches he had sewn. Then he looked at me accusingly. "You told me about everything, but you forgot to tell me about taking out the stitches!" I apologized and asked him to tell me about it. Barry grinned. "The doctor told me it wouldn't hurt, but I told him I didn't believe him. He had awful big scissors so I told him I'd yell. He told me I could if I wanted to, but it didn't hurt! I was kinda scared, but it really didn't hurt. It felt funny, but it didn't hurt. The doctor said I was great!"

Everything was in Barry Price's favor. He was strong and psychologically healthy before the surgery. The procedure was uncomplicated. His parents were supportive but didn't infantilize him. The hospital staff was medically and psychologically sophisticated. And Barry was prepared to cope actively with the experience.

Very often children are not as quick to share their fantasies and fears as Barry was, and unless we make the effort to elicit their feelings we will have no idea what is especially or idiosyncratically upsetting to the child. I've known children who believed if a doctor looked inside them the doctor would "be able to see bad things" the children had done. I knew a girl who, after returning from a hospital stay for minor surgery, developed a terror of going to sleep at night. Her fear turned out to be based on the fantasy that if she weren't awake and able to identify herself, some nurse or doctor might come and mistake her for someone else and operate on her again.

We know that young children have fears of separation, helplessness, and castration. We know they have confused or erroneous ideas about their bodies. But beyond that we must work hard to hear and be responsive to the fantasies and ideas each child experiences. I say work hard, for without active support it is rare for young children to be able to express the content of their fantasies. They will express themselves behaviorally—showing us their anger, fearfulness, withdrawal, and neediness—but they won't tell us why they are acting the way they are. Often they aren't consciously aware of what has precipitated their behavior, and at such times it can be useful for adults to share with children their own remembered fantasies and conceptions from childhood. When I work with hospitalized children I usually say, "When I was little I used to think that . . ." and the child will respond with "Really!" or "So you thought that too!" or even, "That's silly! I don't think that anymore!" Then we can talk about the silly or scary ideas kids have, correct any misconceptions, and facilitate their active, aware participation in their healing. It takes effort, but it is necessary, worthwhile effort.

Vera Lane was nineteen when the car in which she was riding was hit by a truck and caught fire. By the time she was rescued she had suffered burns over thirty percent of her body as well as fractures of her right ankle, leg, and wrist. Her girl friend who had been driving dragged herself out of the car despite a broken pelvis and then went back to help Vera. The truck driver was dead.

In my initial involvement in this case, I heard about Vera only incidentally. I was called in to work with the wife and children of the truck driver. Four months later Vera's parents called to request help for Vera and themselves. Amanda and Stuart Lane described a horrendous four months. "When we were called to the hospital we couldn't believe it. They wouldn't let us see her at all that first day, but they gave us her ring and we knew it was true." Mrs. Lane was clutching her husband's arm. "When they did let us see her, God forgive me, I almost wished they hadn't." She began to sob and Mr. Lane continued in a hoarse whisper. "Vera is our only child. We tried for years, and when she finally came it was like a miracle. I was thirty-nine and Amanda was thirty-six. We never thought it would happen, but it did and Vera has been our golden child. She was so beautiful and talented, so full of life and laughter." He pulled a picture out of his wallet to show me. Vera had been beautiful, stunningly so. "When we saw her it just wasn't Vera. Her face and arms and chest were so horribly burned. We couldn't see how badly then, she was all bandaged, but God help us, we've seen it a hundred times since. We prayed for her to live, oh, how we prayed! But knowing now what she's gone through and what's ahead of her, I don't know if we were right. Vera doesn't think so, she just lies there, bearing the pain and whimpering, 'Why didn't you just let me die?'

"At first we all struggled to keep her alive—the doctors talked about fluid loss and some chemical balance or another, and the danger of infection. We had to go into her room all covered up with sterile masks and gowns. They didn't want us there, but they couldn't stop us. And she did get infected and they had to do horrible things to her. They explained it to us, and to her. But when they scraped away the dead skin and she'd scream through the painkillers, we wanted to die. We couldn't do anything but be there. It's different now. Now she faces months and months of skin grafts and plastic surgery and physical therapy, and there's still nothing we can do but be there. She doesn't want us, she doesn't want the plastic surgery, she doesn't want anything. We're desperate!''

I listened to their agony without interrupting. I wanted to believe that my silence was appropriate—they needed to talk and to be heard. I also knew that my mouth was so dry I could barely speak. All of us have our own fears and horrors; mine is fire. I knew and felt what the Lanes were saying. I'd once worked with badly burned patients and I could still hear the screams and smell the stench of burned, infected flesh. And I knew the depression that accompanies the combination of prolonged hospitalization, bodily mutilation, and seemingly endless surgeries. I also knew the burn unit where Vera had been treated. It was one of the best; the team of plastic surgeons who would be performing the grafts and reconstructions were expert. And finally, I knew the months and months of hard, painful, frustrating work Vera would have to put in to regain the use of her hands. So I knew; now what?

I said to the Lanes, "I can understand your desperation. Just listening to you I can feel some of it myself, and I don't even know Vera. Her desperation and depression are more than understandable, they're a reaction to the massive insults her body and mind have taken since the accident. She may really want to die, or she may be feeling so helpless and hopeless she anticipates nothing good or safe ahead of her. If she is willing to see me, I may be able to help her cope better. I would hope so. She can also be helped if both of you are able to deal better with what has happened and will happen to her. There I feel more assured. You are here and you say you want to help. That's all we need to become therapeutic allies for Vera. If we could just get her to fight, to cry, to get angry, anything! We can't reach her when she just lies there. Mrs. Lane, you've raised a crucial point. It would help me to know what Vera was like before the accident. Was she a fighter?''

"In some ways, yes. She loved tennis and was very competitive. She certainly fought us when we wanted her to go to college and she wanted to be a photographer. She won, too. She was probably right, for it took her only a month to get a job with a newspaper as a photographer. In less than year she's gotten two raises and now she always gets a by-line—always *got* a by-line.'' Tears began streaming down her face. "You know, I just remembered. When Vera was seven she broke her ankle and had to be in a cast. It was impossible to keep her in bed. She'd hop around on one foot, getting into her usual mischief. She made a game of it. She even insisted on walking to school on crutches; she wouldn't let me drive her. Yes, she used to be a fighter.''

Stu Lane nodded. "Mrs. Kliman, I've been doing a lot of thinking. You saw how beautiful Vera was. She knew it, but it never seemed very important to her. She was always more interested in other people's faces. That's one of the things that made her such a fine photographer, her skill in getting expressions and finding beauty where no one else saw it. It has me so confused. If she'd been a vain girl who depended on her looks, I could better understand her attitude. But she was never vain. She liked being pretty, but she never used her looks to get anything. Now she's totally preoccupied with how ugly she is. I don't understand it.''

"I'm not sure I do either, Mr. Lane, but perhaps Vera's feelings have less to do with the loss of her looks than with the loss of the sense of herself. We get used to our faces and the way we look. It becomes a part of us. When our bodies are mutilated, we *feel* mutilated. She has also suffered severe damage to her hands, and her hands have been most important to her whether for using a camera or wielding a tennis racket. Now she's not the same—her body, face, and hands have become scarred, painful, and alien, and they no longer serve her. But with all that, I am encouraged to hear she was a fighter before. It makes it more possible to bring her back.''

Amanda Lane nodded slowly. ''Alien, that's the word. She's alien to herself. I've never admitted it even to myself, but she's alien to me. She doesn't look or feel or sound like my child. I *know* she is, but it doesn't *feel* as if she is. That sounds crazy! Mothers are supposed to know their own child no matter what.''

''You're describing a reality,'' I told Mrs. Lane, ''not anything crazy. Because Vera looks, feels, and acts differently, you both have lost reliable points of reference. Over the past nineteen years you've learned to relate to your daughter, consciously and unconsciously, according to the signals given. Now the signals have been radically changed and you are both lost. One of our jobs is to find a new set of signals so you and she can find each other again. Since you agree Vera feels alien to herself it would be helpful if you could share with her your own sense of alienation. As upsetting as such an acknowledgment might be, it would be a first step in working on the existing situation.''

I waited as the Lanes looked at each other. Stu Lane touched his wife gently under the chin, then they both nodded sadly. He said, ''I think I could do that. At the beginning we had no idea what to expect—even what to hope for. The doctors just told us we'd have to wait. Now we know. She will be able to make it, but it's going to be such a long, hard road. They showed us drawings of what she'd look like— many drawings, because they didn't know how she *wanted* to look. They can't make her face exactly like it was before, but she won't be ugly. Even her hands will be all right. Not completely, but good enough to use. But she won't look at the pictures, Mrs. Kliman. It makes me angry, but I can't tell her that.''

"Why not? Six months ago if she'd given up on something important to her, given up without even trying, wouldn't you have gotten angry? Wouldn't you have told her so?''

"Sure, but she wasn't hurt then.''

"But now that she *is* hurt she needs your caring, your support, and, when appropriate, your anger all the more. You're her father, and she needs to know you still love her enough to act like her father. And if your anger should stimulate her to get angry too, that would help her a lot more than her depression.''

"But she's entitled to be depressed. Look what's happened to her.''

"Of course she is. But she's still got choices. She needs support to be depressed because she has so much to be depressed about, but she also needs support to be angry, to fight, to yell, to make decisions that will restore her to a full life. We can't do that for her, but we can help her to want it for herself.''

We were all tired by now, but not nearly as tired as we were to become over the next eleven months, months made up of thousands of hours of painful struggling, agonizing setbacks, and glorious successes.

My first session with Vera was rough on us both. When I entered her room she greeted me with, "Hideous, aren't I?''

"No, Vera, you're not, but the scars certainly are. What are you planning to do about them?''

She turned away. "Nothing, there's nothing I can do. What a stupid question! Just leave me alone, I don't want to talk.''

"That's one choice you have. You could do nothing and live the rest of your life hidden behind hideous scars.''

"The rest of my life, ha! I don't want the rest of my life. I wish I were dead."

"That's another choice you have. You could die and not have to make any more decisions . . . or have any more opportunities. It would be wasteful, but it's another choice."

"You don't know me, so you don't know what I want."

"That's why I'm asking you what *you* really want."

The scars couldn't hide the stricken look on her face. "I want to go back in time. I want it to be before. And it can't be, so I don't want anything!"

"What would you want to go back to, Vera? If we could turn back time, what would you want to be?"

"I'd want to be me. I'd want to be back at the paper to see my work in print. I'd want to get tired because I did so much, not because I hurt so much." She began to sob. "Damn why, why do you make me think of what's impossible?"

"Because it's not impossible. You don't know *what* you can do, or what can be done to help you be yourself again." Vera reached for a tissue next to her bed. She could only use the middle two fingers of her right hand. She raised the Kleenex and dabbed at her face. "That's what I mean, Vera. Two months ago you couldn't even use two fingers. . . ."

"Big deal! I can use two fingers, what does that get me?"

"It's not a big deal, but it's a beginning. It gets you the independence of not having to have someone wipe your nose for you. It's a step in a long series of steps that will lead you back to being yourself . . . and ahead to what you want to be."

"I'm so tired, tired of the pain, tired of the hassling, tired of this endless prison my body has become."

"Vera, I'd think you were unreal if you weren't tired. You're entitled to be. But you're also entitled to use all the help you can get. The doctors have told your parents that plastic surgery will remove almost all of your scarring, that you can have a face that you can live comfortably with—a face you can in good part design yourself, a face not terribly different from the one you had. They also said you can regain nearly complete use of both hands—certainly enough to continue your work, probably even your tennis. But only if you're willing to work at it. Everybody seems to think you are worth the effort. What do you think?''

"I don't know what to think. I'm so scared. I don't know what I'm worth anymore. Do you know how terrifying that is?''

"If you're asking if I can put myself exactly in your position, probably not. But if you're asking me whether I know what it's like to be terrified when my body doesn't work as I'm used to it working, then yes. That I know. I believe it's possible to accept and even like oneself despite the most terrible, painful experiences. Think about it, Vera. I'd like to see you again soon. Will you call me?''

"Perhaps. I'll think about it.''

It took two weeks for Vera to call. During that time she did a great deal of thinking, crying, questioning, and raging. So did her parents. As a result Vera *demanded* a consultation with the plastic surgeons she had been avoiding. I met one of them in the hall later that month. He shook his head. "You know, that poor sweet kid has changed into a rotten little bitch." I grinned. "Dr. Simpson, I'm delighted to hear it! The poor sweet kid was lying there in frozen misery. Now the rotten little bitch has begun to fight for herself and the quality of her life, and I couldn't be more pleased.''

The next months weren't easy for any of us, especially not for Vera and her parents. The bitchiness subsided, but there were still times of anger, frustration, and despondency. But also of accomplishment and even rejoicing. The staff complained about how difficult she often was, but they grew fond of her and maintained a balance between supporting her and making her support herself. Her parents learned to know when gentle acceptance and firm prodding would be most helpful. Vera gradually learned to be at ease with her new face, even with the hairline scars that remained. She sweated through her hand exercises and cried and swore when she couldn't meet her goal for the week, but she also shouted with glee when she got ahead of herself. In the seventh month of her hospitalization she demanded that her mother bring one of her cameras to her room, and with that we knew she was going to make it. For the next weeks, often disguised in mask and gown, Vera spent every spare moment slipping into the doctors' lounge, the nurses' station, the physical therapy gym, the pediatric ward—any place she had access to—to snap pictures. On her last day at the hospital she presented the staff with a thick album—forty pages of portraits. The faces they showed were gentle, happy, crying, straining, angry, worried, pouting, grinning, sweating, dazed, and fearful. Her album was entitled "Sight and Insight."

All of us involved with Vera Lane would have to say that the months of strain, pain, and work were well worth it. But it's important not to underestimate the toll these months took or the importance of the mutual support system that evolved among her care-givers. Vera's depression in the early months was highly contagious—it infected her parents and the hospital staff. Her spirit—angry or cooperative—was also contagious. Certainly the frequent informal discussions various staff members had with one another were helpful as "safety valves." Twice a month the staff also met in formal conference for an hour and a half, to share not clinical management but their feelings about Vera (and other long-term patients). From these meetings they gained mutual support. (When hospital staff members, no matter what their discipline or expertise, feel alone in their frustration, irritation, fatigue, or lack of accomplishment, they cannot serve their patients well. Relatively few hospitals utilize their regularly scheduled staff meetings to meet the staff's own psychological needs. Despite pressures of time and money, it is clear to me that such support systems are crucial to comprehensive patient care, and to optimal performance of hospital personnel.)

Vera's eventual recovery was a tribute not only to the skill of her care-givers, but also to the reservoir of strengths she had amassed over nineteen years of active, productive living prior to her accident. As drained as these resources were by the severity of her pain and mutilation, they were available to her as she reconstructed her life. Perhaps Vera's greatest vulnerability was the loss of her sense of self—her feelings of alienation from herself and from others. As she struggled in a pained body that no longer functioned in the ways she had long identified as hers, she became increasingly disorganized and depressed. It was as if she had been catapulted into a world utterly foreign to her, inside and outside. She began to identify with her mutilation when she could no longer identify with herself. She expressed this clearly when she greeted me with, "Hideous, aren't I?" Therapeutic intervention began when I differentiated between the injury and the person who received the injury—"You're not, but the scars certainly are." As Vera gradually regained her sense of self, she began to rage against the restraints and agonies the injuries had imposed upon her. This anger served her well as it fueled her aggressive and reconstructive attempts at healing. The bitchier she got, the more energetically she engaged herself in regaining the use of her hands and designing a new face for herself. It has been my observatiion, and the observation of many clinicians, that the more compliant, passive, and depressed patients are, the more slowly they heal and the more secondary infections and side effects they suffer. Each of Vera's accomplishments served to reestablish and augment her sense of self. Her gift of photographs to the staff was a statement: I have found myself, I am worthy, I have something valuable to share.

A case that illustrates the multiple problems of hospitalization for diagnostic purposes followed by major surgery happens to be the only case in this book in which the patient can be identified. That is because I was the patient.

Many years ago, following a seemingly inconsequential fall, I developed a backache. I was annoyed and uncomfortable, but not very concerned. Anyone who totes young children around, gardens, lugs laundry, and sits for hours at a desk gets accustomed to minor backaches. But this one didn't stay minor. Within several weeks the pain became so severe that I could neither sit nor walk for more than a few minutes. The only way I could be comfortable was to lie flat on the floor. My husband, Gil, had been nagging me to see an orthopedist, but I didn't "have the time . . . besides, it'll go away." Such denial did not serve me well. Several days later I noticed my right leg was swinging widely when I walked, producing a pronounced limp. Now I became worried. I went to an orthopedist who examined and X-rayed me carefully. His diagnosis: probable herniated disk, requiring traction for one month. The long-range prognosis was worse—probable surgery to remove the disk and fuse the two vertebrae together, such surgery to be followed by six months in bed in a body cast. "Impossible!" I told him. I had three young children. There was no way I would allow myself to be separated from them for so long. I limped out of his office scared, depressed, and hurting. I was going to lick this myself! I could get a traction pulley at a local surgical supply house, Gil could rig it up to the bed, and I could use it several hours a day and all night. That would do it.

Gil was skeptical. I got annoyed. He was a psychiatrist, not an orthopedist, so what did he know! He knew enough to recognize my anxiety and my denial. Gently but firmly he insisted that I consult with another orthopedist and a neurosurgeon who specialized in back injuries. He reminded me that self-treatment is lousy treatment and asked if I would agree to let him act so cavalierly if he had the back injury. That did it. Two days later he accompanied me to a famous teaching hospital for an outpatient consultation.

I was examined by two specialists. They agreed I should have a myelogram to confirm their diagnosis of a herniated disk. I gasped at the thought. A myelogram! My God, that huge needle, injected into *my* spine! The neurologist told me that there was already considerable damage to the sciatic nerve and without treatment I might lose the use of my right leg. Now I was terrified. I began to cry. I asked them to tell me in detail what would have to be done if the myelogram were positive, how long I would have to be hospitalized, and how long I would have to convalesce. They were as thorough in their explanations as they had been in their examinations. They suggested immediate hospitalization, but when I said I had three children to prepare for my absence, ages seven, six, and three, they agreed to admit me three days later. Gil drove me home. I spent the trip writing copious notes to myself (my organization was an attempt to overcome the overwhelming sense of helplessness I felt). And crying.

At dinner I began to explain to my children what was going to happen as it had been explained to me. (I ate standing up, the car ride had been so agonizing.) The kids were wide-eyed. Jodie, then seven, asked if I would have to have an operation; Steven, six, asked me to show him where; and David, three, wanted to know who would take care of him and "how many sleeps" I'd be away. I told them I'd be in the hospital at least two weeks, more likely three. I promised they could come visit me almost every day if they wanted to, and could call me anytime. I assured them that Chris—our warm, loving au pair girl—would take good care of them, as would their daddy. I prepared them for the fact that I would look different in the hospital, probably much paler, and wouldn't be feeling very good some of the time, but then I added firmly that the hospital would make me better so I could again play with them. I sounded a lot more convincing than I felt. As they told me three weeks later, my anxiety leaked through.

The next two days were taken up with dozens of details I'd usually accomplished without thinking. Friends and relatives were notified and put on call in case of emergency. The pantry and freezer were stocked—enough to last for months. I made a calendar for each child so days could be marked off while I was gone. Gil suggested I make a tape for David, who was accustomed to a bedtime ritual of one story and two songs before sleep—twenty-one days' worth. And I read every medical journal and textbook on herniated disks I could find. I wasn't terribly happy with what I learned. In fact the only thing I felt good about was my choice of doctors. Extremely experienced, they urged early patient activity, short hospitalization, body corsets (removable) rather than plaster casts, and full explanations.

I entered the hospital as prepared as possible, but I was still frightened. I also was depressed and furious with myself. Why hadn't I paid attention to my symptoms earlier—maybe I could have avoided the myelogram and the surgery. If only I hadn't been so stubborn. "If only." I thought how many hundreds of times I had heard that from others. Yet I expected a great deal more of myself (forgetting that intellectual awareness does not necessarily transform behavior or feelings).

The myelogram was fully as anxiety-provoking and, later, as painful as I had been led to believe. No matter how much I trusted the physicians, that monstrously huge needle entering my spine scared the hell out of me. But I followed orders carefully. Under *no circumstances* was I to lift my head for twenty-four hours. I didn't, but I still got a blinding headache. Worse yet, the test proved positive.

My orthopedic surgeon reexplained what would be done. An incision would be made, the disk removed, and bone chips would be grafted from my hip and used to fuse two vertebrae together. There would be a great deal of post-surgical pain. Since I had a sensitivity to morphine and codeine and Demerol, the anesthetist would have to experiment to find which painkillers I could tolerate. I was pleased my doctor shared his concern with me, but I remained frightened. He acknowledged my fear, said it was appropriate, but added that I would receive the finest care possible. I knew that, but I was still scared.

The operation was a success. All I remember about it is receiving the preoperative medication, the endless ride in elevators and down halls—and then pain. Unbelievable, overwhelming, terrifying pain. And total helplessness. Weaving in and out of consciousness over the next twenty-four hours, I found myself unable to move a muscle. I learned later that Gil was with me constantly, but I was aware only of how desperately I hurt. I cried and pleaded for medicine. I also pleaded to be released from the straps that held me immobile. (That was the *one* thing my physician forgot to prepare me for.) I half remember nurses explaining I had to be kept completely still so I wouldn't disturb the bone fusion, but still I begged. They held my hand, spoke softly, and were exquisitely kind to the regressed baby I had become. I couldn't take anything by mouth and vomited shortly after each shot. Four nurses held me so I wouldn't destroy the fusion, but vomit still covered me and my bed. Patiently and repeatedly they cleaned me. I was disgusted and horrified—why couldn't I stop vomiting, it hurt so, I felt so sick. Why couldn't anyone help me!

Sometime that night I fell asleep. The pain woke me. I found I couldn't breathe—I tried to yell, but no sound came. My nurse must have hit the emergency signal because the suddenly the room was full of people. I couldn't talk, couldn't breathe, couldn't open my eyes. But I could hear. "No reaction. . . . Can't get a pulse. . . . She's cold. . . .

My God! She's dead, you idiot. . . . Move over. . . . Give me . . . cc's. . . ."

No! No! I screamed inside myself. I am not dead. Don't leave me. Don't let me die. I'm alive. Help me! But I knew there was no sound. Then there was nothing.

The next morning I awoke again to extreme pain. The day nurse was on and I asked her what had happened. She assured me I was all right. She didn't know anything had happened. I asked to see my orthopedic surgeon and was told he'd be in later. I asked to see my neurosurgeon; he'd be in tomorrow. I asked to see my chart. "Now, now, you know that's against the rules!" I asked to see the floor resident. "He's busy now." I started to cry. "I want to see my husband. I demand you call Dr. Kliman immediately. His number is pasted to the phone." (I still was not allowed to move anything but my eyes and mouth.) "Now, dear, you know he'll be in at noon. Be a good girl now and just rest. Would you like your bath now? It'll be so refreshing." "No, I want to see my husband. If you don't call him I'll scream." I opened my mouth and she clamped her hand over it. "Now stop it, you're acting like a baby!" And indeed, I felt as helpless as a baby. Passively, overwhelmed, I lay there. She washed me gently, keeping up a steady stream of chatter, telling me what a good girl I was being. What choice did I have!

In a while the resident made his usual morning visit. I asked him what had happened during the night. He turned away and said, "What do you mean? Nothing happened." "Doctor, I *know* something happened last night. I felt it, I heard it. Now tell me!" "All that happened was you had a nightmare. It's not unusual to have nightmares when you are heavily medicated, but nothing happened." And he left the room.

At that moment I couldn't tell which was more terrifying, the pain or the feeling that I was going crazy! I knew something had happened. The nurse and the resident had said it was a nightmare, but I knew it wasn't. Either they were crazy or I was.

Gil came in at noon. As he bent over to kiss me I begged him to get the nurse out of the room. He asked her if she would be kind enough to get him some juice as he was going to miss lunch. She left saying she would get him a tray. I told Gil what I remembered and what I had been told. I said I was afraid I was having a psychotic episode (amazing how loving support facilitates a return from regression), or something terrible really had happened the night before. He immediately phoned my physician and received permission to review my chart. I wasn't dreaming, I wasn't psychotic. The chart was clear. I had gone into shock, the nurse had called the emergency team, and I had been given noradrenaline, a blood transfusion, and oxygen—and I had recovered.

Emergency medical treatment: superb. Psychological first aid: inadequate, inappropriate, and damaging.

When I saw the children that evening I looked and felt physically awful, but psychologically I was euphoric. I could have died; medical expertise had saved me, and hurting or not, I was elated to be alive and sane. The nurse's aid brought in milk and cookies, and while the children ate I asked them about their day. Steve told me a neighbor had taken them to see *Snow White* that afternoon. I said, "That's a scary movie, weren't you scared?" Jodie rather disdainfully informed me, "It's just a movie, it's not real!" Steve nodded, "When I got scared Jodie held my hand and told me it was just pretend, so I wasn't really scared—very much." David's mouth was stuffed with cookies. "How about you, Davy, were you scared?" He looked at me in surprise, "I don't know, Mommy, I fell asleep." It hurt to laugh, but I did, It felt great to be worrying about my kids instead of myself.

The rest of my hospital stay and recuperation was rapid

and uneventful. What I learned from this firsthand experience has been essential to my work with patients and hospital staffs. Patients (and nonpatients) exercise a lot of initial denial. We are fearful of what will happen to us in the hospital and are frequently embarrassed by our fears. Pain makes us feel helpless, and when we regress we are temporarily unable to function maturely. We need to know what to expect, we need to understand what we are experiencing. Protecting us from unpleasant reality only increases our inability to cope with it. The resident's decision to infantilize me, to placate me with a story so I wouldn't be frightened, deprived me of my right to know about my body. My own surgeons, on the other hand, were willing to, even insistent on discussing my "shock" episode so I could gain mastery over it. They serve as models of the skillful physicians who treat people, not illnesses.

A Time of Scapegoats

5

Only thirty years ago divorce was a rare occurrence, considered either an indulgence of the rich and eccentric or the final alternative of the inhumanly abused. Today it is elected by more than one family in three. It prevails over a broad economic cross section and can be based on any of myriad claims of incompatibility. Whether or not one approves of divorce is irrelevant: it has become one of our most common human realities, with the families affected posing a problem and challenge to our social structure, even a matter of public mental health. We can see the effects around us, in burgeoning singles clubs and magazines, a new emphasis on apartment living, single-parent organizations, and an astonishing increase in legal specialization and overburdened court calendars.

In this broadened arena, issues of alimony, child support, child custody, and allowance for sexual activity during and after divorce proceedings are no longer automatically decided; more and more, they are left open for reappraisal. A couple that accepts these options honestly and responsibly has a good chance of resettling its split family in healthy and productive new lives. *How* a couple divorces can prove more crucial than the decision to divorce, for like any social contract, divorce demands respectful understanding and a willingness to be creative. Unfortunately, the majority of divorces are neither respectful nor creative. As is true of so many marriages, they are prompted by neurotic, magical, escapist, or denigrating motives often related to experiences lived through years before and now projected on the marital partner. The fairy-tale notion of marriage is that "they lived happily ever after," but in real life happiness is a goal accomplished only by daily work and understanding. Yet how few of us on the threshold of marriage understand this. We simply assume that marriage itself will solve our problems, will *make* us happy. So when our marriage breaks apart we feel bereft, angry, righteously aggrieved. And all too often we feel we have failed, that we are now unloved and unlovable. With such a massive loss of self-esteem, is it any wonder that we attempt to drag down with us those we have loved?

I have no illusions about stemming the tide of divorce in our time. It will take generations for society to understand what all too few people yet realize, that marriage is a contract not only to "love, honor, and cherish," but also to work, grow, and learn—to adapt to the jigsaw puzzle of changes, challenges, losses, and gains inherent in any close relationship between two people. Once this is popularly grasped, we will see fewer innocent marriages and many fewer destructive divorces. But until such near-Utopian time, we must pay attention to those people most vulnerable.

It is almost impossible to list all types of high-risk marriages. Included would be couples who have lost a child by death; couples who married in adolescence; couples who used marriage as an escape; couples who are themselves children of divorced parents; couples "forced" to marry by unplanned pregnancy, family, or peer pressure; and couples bombarded by multiple or overwhelming stresses. There is nothing inevitably destructive in these circumstances, but such couples do run a higher risk of divorce than does the general population. I have known some who mastered their vulnerability and emerged stronger and better able to derive gratification from marriage, but I have known many more so programmed by both their life history and their maladaptive marital relationship that they unconsciously precipitated their own divorce, even while protesting that they had no choice. Such people seek to set up situations in which their expectation of being abandoned pushes their partners into abandoning them. An accusation is made and is established as a position. It is extraordinarily difficult to be responsive and loving to a spouse whose constant refrain is: "You don't love me." "You never really loved me." "You care only about your work." "You only want sex." "You never want sex." And so on.

Sexual problems are the most common complaints presented to clinicians and lawyers in divorce cases, but usually the sexual issue is a red herring—or at most a symptom of some greater underlying problem in the ongoing process of relating to a spouse. Whoever originated the epigram "The primary sexual organ is the brain" deserves great credit. Except in relatively rare cases of organic damage or disease, most sexual dysfunction is a result of ignorance, fear, insecurity, or social patternings—all stemming from or related to concepts of marriage roles formed in childhood. One would think that with all the frankness of sex education, at school and in the home, children today would have a better chance for sexual happiness than did past generations, but the fact is that for all children are taught of sex, they are taught virtually nothing of *sexuality*. Whereas sex is an act, a manifestation of a psychophysical urge, sexuality is a biological given influenced by society. It is much like speech. Infants are born with the ability to make sounds, but it takes years of imitat-

ing, listening, and learning before the babbling becomes useful, articulate language; without those years of nurturing,
speech remains immature and often inarticulate. By the same
token, if parents concerned themselves with teaching and
modeling mature sexuality—along with respectful interpersonal relations—children could grow up comfortable with
their biological selves, secure in their self-esteem and respectful of others' individuality. Possessed of such a solid
sense of self, we can handle disappointment or being hurt
without reacting violently or vindictively; we can respond
with adapative appropriateness. Most importantly, we can be
sure of ourselves before we commit ourselves to another, for
we will recognize whatever complex of wishes can be
gratified by that commitment. Loving is enough only when
we can empathize with both our anticipated partner and ourselves.

Marion and Milton Cramer sat in my office and shared
their concern about what their impending divorce would do to
their children—Elliot, age eleven, and Ruth, five. It was the
only thing they shared, other than a driving wish for immediate divorce. After thirteen years of marriage the best
either could say of the other was that he or she "is not a bad
parent." They had, after all, never argued in front of the
children, they had always presented "a united front" on
matters of discipline and privileges (no matter how loudly
they fought about it "privately"), and "under no circumstances have we ever burdened the children with our
disagreements about finances, friends, entertainment, sexual
preferences, or even politics."

During our first fifteen minutes together, I heard much
of what the children must have overheard for years. "She
overindulges Elliot." "He pays no attention to Elliot."
"She's extravagant and irresponsible about money." "He's
so tight he wouldn't even buy Elliot a decent sled." "She
acts like sex is an unpleasant duty." "He uses me like he

uses his toothbrush, I'm just another piece of equipment for his physical needs." "She never appreciates how hard I work." "Nothing I ever do is good enough for him."

I interrupted their tirade. "You've made it very clear how disappointed and angry you are at each other. Since you both insist you have no interest in preserving your marriage and are here only to get counseling for your children, I would like to hear about your own childhoods and life experiences. The more I understand about you, the better I can help you to help your children."

As their stories unfolded, I was impressed by how ingeniously they had chosen partners who could help them relive their unhappiest childhood experiences. Milton Cramer was the next to youngest of ten children of immigrant parents. By the time he came along there was little parental nurture left for him, and this was soon diluted by birth of still another brother when Milton was sixteen months old. His mother performed her duties: the house was spotless, the children's clothes were clean and pressed, and meals were hot. Milton's mothering came mostly from a sister sixteen years his senior. His father did a father's job—he worked hard to support his family, to provide dowries for his three daughters—and he put aside a bit for each son's education. The boys were expected to work to make up the rest, and work they all did. There was no time for father-son talks, much less games. A bright boy, and determined to meet his parents' expectations, Milton Cramer worked two jobs through high school and still managed to win a scholarship to college. Sadly, neither of his parents lived to see him graduate. He got his degree, went on to graduate school on another scholarship and got another degree, but he never got his parents' seal of approval. They taught him well the value of work, education, and responsibility; they were just too burdened to offer him the rest of parenting, or to model for him the affection he learned years later they had had for each other.

Marion Cramer's background was ostensibly very different, but psychologically it was just as barren. Her father simply disappeared from her life when she was five. Her mother, depressed and vengeful, was singularly unable to empathize with her daughter's needs, either psychological or developmental. She did, however, fill her daughter's life with art lessons, piano lessons, party dresses, trips, cultural events—and bitterness. A day rarely passed without allusions to "that man" and his "lack of decency," his infidelity, irresponsibility, and vulgarity, his "false face" and "unspeakable conduct." Marion Cramer learned her lessons well: "Men are only out for what they can get." But she was puzzled. She remembered her father very differently than did her mother. Marion recalled him as a huge, happy, affectionate man. "I must have been too young to really know," she concluded.

The Cramers were enmeshed in powerful unconscious forces. At last able to turn from passive to active, they were doing to their children what had been done to them. It was no accident that Mrs. Cramer had pushed so hard for divorce when her daughter was exactly the age she had been when she lost her father. She was unconsciously caught in an anniversary reaction. Never having been allowed to grieve openly for the father who left her, she had to repeat her circumstances in order to get another chance to master her loss—only this time it would be through her daughter.

I shared my observations with the Cramers: how clever they were in meeting each other's most dreaded expectations, and how inept they were in accepting from each other the approval, appreciation, and affection each wanted so desperately. Despite their expressions of protest I plunged ahead. "However you decide to resolve your own problems is up to you. But as a Child Advocate I must tell you that the way in which you resolve your situation will have direct effect upon your children. They already have to deal with a reality—their father has been out of the house for two weeks—yet neither of you has openly and clearly told them what is going on. Mrs. Cramer, you've informed them their father was on a business trip. Yet during this supposed trip you say you and your husband had a violent argument in the living room after the children were in bed. It's more than likely that Elliot and Ruth overheard that argument—as they must have been overhearing your arguments for years. How are they going to be able to understand what is real and what is not real when you deny their perceptions? How will they be able to sustain trust in either of you when you lie to them? Neither of them is mature, physically or emotionally, yet you are forcing them to deal with adult problems all alone, without the adult support they need and deserve. Being children, they believe that *they* are responsible for your problems and arguments. In reality, they are the victims.''

"But if we tell them their father has left for good and we're getting a divorce, won't that frighten them?'' Mrs. Cramer asked. ''Won't it make them insecure?''

"I'd be surprised if they were not already feeling frightened and insecure. But at least they can respond to what you tell them, they can question. And they can be helped to deal with the situation. It might even be a relief for them to know that you'd both be happier apart, that they aren't to blame for your problems.''

Over the next three months I found out just how frightened and worried Elliot and Ruth were. As a child at the Oedipal stage, Ruth was very vulnerable. She was convinced ''Mommy sent Daddy away because I love him more than I love her.'' (Every Oedipal child loves the opposite-sex parent ''more''; it is developmentally appropriate.) Terrified of what she saw as her mother's vindictiveness, she suffered from nightmares (about witches), was constantly in the nurse's office at school complaining of headaches, and had become accident-prone.

I interpreted the nightmares as projections of anger upon

the "bad" witches and expressions of fear of her "bad" mommy. As Mrs. Kramer began to empathize with Ruthie and to understand her daughter's feelings, without having to retaliate, the nightmares disappeared. The headaches and trips to the nurse were played out with dolls and puppets. One day during a session Ruthie was piling books on a doll's head. Mrs. Cramer remarked, "Ruthie, you're putting too many books on that doll's head, you'll squash her." Mr. Cramer looked shocked as he said, "Marion! I think we've both put too much on that child's head!" Ruthie *appeared* not to have heard her father's interpretation, but continued her play with the doll—of going to the nurse, being sent home, and having her mommy take care of her in a gentle, loving manner. I kept up a running monologue, commenting on what the "doll" was feeling and doing, occasionally connecting the doll and "little girls who feel so burdened, lonely, and scared." This game and others like it were played out many times until, by the end of the second month, Ruth's headaches had virtually disappeared. The accidents were handled similarly; Ruth was brought to see that she was punishing herself for her "bad" thoughts, finding it easier to cry about a skinned knee or sprained finger than about her scary "missing" feelings. Eventually, she was able to acknowledge them correctly by telling her mother, "When Daddy isn't here and I miss him I want a cookie *and* I want to phone him right away!"

Elliot presented only one troubling symptom. Until a year ago, he had been an honor student. Now he was failing math, the subject he used to enjoy most. As with so many children exposed to long periods of family secrets and denials of observable reality, Elliot had transposed his parents' injunctions not to ask questions, not to "know" what was going on, into an injunction not to learn. That he chose not to learn math was striking. I made a working hypothesis about Elliot's mathematics inhibition. In part it was an act of self-punishment, to give up on his favorite subject; in part it was a brilliant symbol for what he was experiencing—things just didn't "add up," his home was "divided," his problems "multiplied," his father was being "subtracted," his whole "set" disrupted, and there were just too many "unknowns." As his parents became better able to talk to Elliot about their feelings and their plans, to help him know that their problems were adult problems and their love for him was independent of their loss of love for each other, Elliot's math improved remarkably. He began talking about his worries and resentments, and his parents in turn were able to hear him and to respond appropriately.

In follow-ups over the past year the progress has continued. The Cramers' divorce is now final; the children, no longer used as pawns or "islands of innocence" are growing well; custody is open, so Mr. Cramer sees his children often and enthusiastically; and both parents have taken responsibility for their own long-term individual problems.

The idea of "staying together for the children's sake" and exposing them to years of stress, vicious arguments, and subtle cruelties does little to facilitate the emotional health of any of the family members. Separation and divorce may well be the healthiest decision in such cases, but only when the parents assume responsibility for what they are doing. With all the anger and resentment that accompanies family breakups, the sense of loneliness and ill treatment, it is hard to resist enlisting children as allies against the other parent. It is also hard, following a divorce, not to hold a mannerism, gesture, or character trait we remember in our ex-spouse against the child who now exhibits it, or not to compete for the love and attention of a child when that child represents the last link to what had been an intense relationship.

It is the parents' obligation not to use or harm their children; and under circumstances that are inevitably harmful, as through a divorce, to assist their children in the most supportive ways possible. It is a task few of us can do well alone. Marion Cramer would have been far less damaged had she received psychological intervention when her father left (and had her mother been able to seek such support). She could have been helped to know that her father had problems not only in being a husband but also in being a daddy, and that his leaving her was not her responsibility or a result of her "badness." He had failed to make her know she was lovable, and realizing this she could then have been taught that all men weren't like her father. She would not have had to seek a man all too willing to confirm her worst expectations, but rather a man whose love she would have been willing to accept, and whom she could love in return.

Remarriage poses special problems for adults and children of all ages. Once separated parents have mastered their feelings about giving each other up, they are ready to invest in a new relationship. And because they are ready, they often assume their children are ready as well. But while the parent has lost a spouse, the child has not lost that spouse as a parent. Thus the child faces an immediate loyalty conflict. If acceptance is given to a stepparent, the original parent will be lost, resentful, angry, or jealous. This is not necessarily the child's fantasy! The original parent may well feel all these things, and more. For not only does that parent have to compete with the ex-spouse's new partner for the children's attention and affection, he or she must also contend with an almost inevitable and intense sense of envy or bitterness that someone should have succeeded where he or she failed. In such situations, children are unable to involve themselves profoundly with the new person; they are still struggling to solve the loyalty conflict they feel (realistically or not) between their original parents. Parents, children, and potential stepparents, all are out of phase with one another at a time of great change and mutual need.

Some children appear to attach themselves rapidly or even immediately to a new person, but this can be deceiving. Such rapid attachment is rarely born out of understanding or judgment, but rather out of anxiety and pressure to conform. There is little we can do to alter or speed up a child's ability to engage himself with a new stepparent, but children can accept and adjust to a parent's need and wish for a new spouse. If children are encouraged to respond to that new person as the parent's spouse, rather than as the children's "instant" parent, the basis of a sound relationship can be established—one that does not have to interfere with or preclude the relationship they have with their original parent. The more we demonstrate to children that we understand their needs, the more children learn to understand and appreciate our needs. Respect and empathy are best gained slowly and by example, rather than by demand.

Shirley Newton consulted me less than a year after her divorce, when her ex-husband was about to remarry. Still stinging from the bitterness of her marriage and its break-up, she was enraged by "that bitch trying to mother *my* children." She wanted to prove to the court that the children's visits to their father and "that woman" were doing psychological damage to the children. "Brenda and George," she assured me, "would be much better off without their father, and certainly should not be exposed to his slut." Rapidly she described the effects on her children: they always returned from their weekly visits cranky, overtired, and filled with junk foods; they expected her "on my lousy child support" to buy them as much as their father did ("I'm always the witch, he's the Santa Claus, and she plays at being Fairy Godmother"); Brenda, age seven, usually threw up after her visits ("And *I'm* the one who has to clean it up"); George, age ten, usually returned angry, hostile, and negativistic ("No matter what I tell him to do, he won't listen. He juts out his chin, just like his father does, and ignores me"). Shirley Newton's complaint ran on: "Worst of all, those two grill the kids about what I do, whom I see, even what I feed them. I won't let my children be used like that! And it's none of their business what I do or don't do!" She concluded her grievances with the request that I write a letter to her lawyer and the Family Court judge stating that in my professional judgment "weekly visits and monthly overnight visits to their father are inflicting grave psychological harm on Brenda and George, and therefore should be terminated immediately."

As I listened, my mind went through all the things I would have liked to say had it not been for my position as her therapist. I thought: Lady, I don't like you! You are angry, manipulative, and abusive. Yes, you probably did get a raw deal, and yes, I do believe you are concerned about your children—but not enough to stop using them as pawns, not enough to think of them as other than instruments of your vengefulness and jealousy. And your ex-husband is probably no better. I pity your kids!

But, after years of analysis and nearly two decades of being a therapist, you don't talk to patients that way. It doesn't help to talk to *anyone* that way. My anger and hostility to Shirley Newton was *my* problem. I was identifying with her own anger, a trap all therapists can fall into. Having made myself aware of these "gut" feelings, I could put them into perspective and allow myself more mature and adaptive interaction. It was true I was worried about her children. I could also hear the pain and the plea behind her anger. That alone relieved my anger and released my empathy.

"Mrs. Newton, I can hear how worried, beset, and angry you feel. Divorces are often brutalizing experiences, and it can take a lot of time and work to get over the taste of bitter failure. You have told me how concerned you are about your children's welfare and behavior, and with good reason.

You have asked me to act in Brenda's and George's behalf, as a Child Advocate, and I am willing to do so. But for me to act intelligently and effectively, I will have to meet with your children, to get to know and understand them. I also will need to learn more about you, and to meet and understand more about Mr. Newton.''

"Oh! Ralph will never agree to see you. He wouldn't even want you to see the children.''

"That may be so, and if it is it will be valuable for me to know it. Still, I would like your permission to call him and ask him to set up an appointment with us. I will tell him, as I tell you now, that whatever either of you say to me is privileged and will not be discussed with the other, or anyone else, without explicit permission. I will also share with him that while you and he no longer have any love or responsibility to one another, you are both still the children's parents, and as such you both have a great deal of responsibility to help them grow and develop in as healthy a way as possible.'' Then I asked Mrs. Newton to tell me about herself, her life before she met her ex-husband, and to give me her reflections on her marriage and divorce.

She had grown up in an angry and frightening home. She said she didn't know which she resented more—her father's alcoholism and abusiveness, or her mother's martyrdom. Even as a young child she used any excuse to get out of the house, and as she grew older she grabbed every new opportunity to be at home as little as possible. An excellent student, she involved herself in many extracurricular activities, both at school and in youth clubs. She also spent "thousands of hours" baby-sitting. Because her father earned a "decent living"—though most of his income went to pay off his bad debts and feed his alcoholism—she was ineligible for a college scholarship. As a result she had to attend what she contemptuously called a "streetcar college" (actually an excellent university) within commuting distance of home. She met her husband shortly after entering college and married him three months later. "Anything to get out of that house." She was not yet eighteen.

Because her husband was in graduate school and their finances were tight, she dropped out of school and took a job to support them. Their agreement, she said with considerable bitterness, was that she would return to finish her education the following year. "But somehow I found myself pregnant." Despite her intelligence and with no religious convictions to the contrary, Mrs. Newton had never thought about birth control of any kind. "It just didn't occur to me I would get pregnant." I mentally filed away this example of cultivated ignorance and innocence, noting her identification with her mother's martyrdom. She then described George's infancy as a difficult time—he was colicky and irritable, she felt exhausted and lonely, and while her husband enjoyed playing with his son and even seemed proud of him, he was jealous of the time and attention the baby demanded.

It was in this period that open warfare began in the Newton household. Mr. Newton felt neglected and unappreciated, Mrs. Newton felt overwhelmed and cheated. As George reached the toddler stage there was a slight improvement. Mr. Newton graduated and got a job he liked. Their financial situation eased as long-standing debts began to be paid off. (Indebtedness was terrifying for Mrs. Newton; it reminded her too vividly of her childhood.) Mrs. Newton began to make plans to return part-time to school, once she could enter George in nursery school, but "somehow again I found myself pregnant." Brenda also proved to be a "difficult baby, subject to attacks of croup and high fevers," and tension again mounted between the Newtons. Mrs. Newton described the following five years as a state of siege—neither of them would give an inch. As her husband began to achieve more, she came to feel more cheated and trapped. Her education again "had to be" postponed. Feeling that her husband was ashamed of her lack of education, she felt ashamed of herself. He criticized her taste in music, art, and literature as romantic or nonsensical. He also criticized her mothering as inept and overprotective. Since he never had problems getting George to listen to him, why should she? He didn't panic when Brenda ran a fever, why did she? And it was the same for their social life. He could carry on informed conversations at parties, why couldn't she?

Their sex life, which had been mutually gratifying during even the troubled earlier years, also became a battleground. If he initiated intercourse and she didn't respond instantly, then she was "frigid." If she initiated it, then she was being "aggressive." She was convinced that only by being cruel to her was he "turned on," and that when he withdrew sexually it was to punish her. After months of battling they both withdrew, and neither approached the other sexually again. Finally he sued for divorce on the grounds of cruel and abusive treatment. He moved out of the house telling the children he couldn't live with "that bitch for one more day." She retaliated with "Good riddance to bad rubbish!"

Although their lawyers were able to intercede through the nastiness of the charges and countercharges, and divorce was eventually granted on grounds of mutual incompatibility, no one interceded for the children.

Mr. Newton was not only willing to consult with me, he called me before I had a chance to call him. When we met, he told much the same story his ex-wife had, but from his point of view. He had grown up in a home where he "never heard" his parents argue, where courtesy and respect were mandatory, and where everyone knew his or her place. His father was, literally and without question, the decision maker and head of the household. Ralph Newton had no memory of ever being touched by his father, except for formal handshakes given upon entering or leaving the house. His mother had attained her college diploma, but she "never used it." She acquiesced to her husband's every wish as was "her duty," and she always put her husband before her children. It thus came as a shock to Mr. Newton to learn by letter just after he had settled in at college that his parents had separated and were getting a divorce. He had always thought them to be so suited to each other. (Again I filed away a thought about *his* cultivated innocence and ignorance.)

He complained to me that his ex-wife had been infantile and immature, unable to be supportive to him when he was overworked, and driving him nearly crazy as she alternated between being a "nympho" or frigid. He pictured her as overanxious and indecisive with the children, and as too "addlepated" to organize her life well enough to continue her education. He also deeply resented her attacks on his fiancée, whom he described as mature, gentle, intelligent, and very fond of Brenda and George. Ralph Newton concluded his grievances with, "And I will not allow her to continue to quiz the children about what I do, how much money I spend, or on what!" (Those poor kids, I thought, are both being used as double agents.) He stated that if his ex-wife attempted in any way to reduce or interfere with his time with his children, he would sue for their custody. "I may well do that anyway," he added almost as an afterthought. "The children would be much better off in a calm, affectionate household, away from her tantrums."

Listening to all the echoes of his ex-wife, I was struck by how similar the needs, conflicts, and retaliatory reactions of these two parents were. If ever children needed an advocate, certainly Brenda and George did, not because their parents didn't love them but because their parents wouldn't see them as people, only as extensions of themselves, or as weapons against the hurtful, insensitive, uncaring ex-spouse.

I gave Mr. Newton the same mini-speech about child advocacy and parental responsibility I had given his ex-wife.

He assured me she would not be willing to cooperate in any therapeutic alliance—and I assured him that getting her cooperation was my responsibility. A temporary truce was set up for a three-month intervention, during which time I would see him and Shirley Newton separately once a week, and the children together also weekly. As the children learned it was safe to talk to me about their worries and anger concerning their parents, and as their parents slowly began to understand how Brenda and George were caught in their cross fire, I was able to get all four Newtons to agree to come together—and those sessions were the most productive of all.

The initial full family sessions were characterized by Mr. and Mrs. Newton's attacks on each other, by Brenda's bursting into tears and covering her ears, and by George's attempting to act as mediator. Finally, in utter helplessness, George shouted, "I hate you both! I don't want to be with either of you! I'll talk to Grandpa and he'll send me away to school." Shirley and Ralph Newton were stunned. For the first time, they were forced to feel one of their children's fury and frustration. Mrs. Newton began to cry and begged George not to run away. Ralph Newton, his voice thick and hoarse, apologized to George for not "understanding" how frightened he was.

From then on everyone worked in the sessions. Brenda talked about how her tummy hurt every time she came home from a visit with her father, and how each time she heard her parents attack each other her stomach "turned over." She also told her mother that Felicia (the fiancée) was "nice" and asked why she couldn't be her "friend," the way she was with Aunt Robin. "You don't mind that Aunt Robin is my friend, do you?" Mrs. Newton explained that Aunt Robin was a relative, so of course she didn't mind. With the concrete logic of a child, Brenda retorted, "But Mrs. Auburn is only a neighbor and you don't mind *her* being my friend!"

With a great deal of support Mrs. Newton was slowly

able to see that Brenda didn't want another mother, though she did want and need Felicia as a friend, just as she needed her father to still be her father. In turn, Mr. Newton ceased his overt attacks on his ex-wife and began to support her mothering capabilities. He also stopped "playing Santa Claus" and spent more of himself with the children, less on toys and treats. He even offered his ex-wife to "return the help you once gave me," to pay her tuition at the college of her choice, an offer that was gladly accepted.

Shirley Newton proved an excellent student, and her self-esteem rose rapidly. Feeling better about herself, she became less vulnerable to the children's panicked manipulations—Brenda's vomiting, George's threats to leave home—and better able to maintain a balance of consistency, caring, and discipline. In response, George began to listen to her. He might still argue or demand, but he accepted (and was relieved by) her firmness. Both parents stopped using the children as spies, and if either had a question or concern, it was expressed by a direct phone call. Close to the end of the intervention Felicia came to see me. She was fond of her fiancé's children, with a high degree of empathy for both, and became an additional and important part of the support system we were building for Brenda and George.

By the end of the third month neither parent still wanted to involve the court in custody or visitation problems. Both agreed to have "open" custody in which the children would live with their mother, but their father could see them "at will," as long as he phoned first. Both parents could see the pitfalls of the arrangement (his last-minute calls at times he knew would be inconvenient, or her refusals to change dates or allow visits for vindictive or manipulative reasons), but while a bit sticky at first, it eventually worked well. I heard from them several times over the next few months, but the calls were to solve problems, not to exacerbate them. Once a Brownie overnight camping trip coincided with Brenda's weekend with her father; he was able to accept an alternate date so she didn't "lose out." Another time Mr. Newton wanted to take the children to Washington, but that meant their losing a day of school; Mrs. Newton was able to understand the value of the trip and got the children their schoolwork in advance.

By the end of two years of follow-ups, life was much smoother and less painful for everyone. Of course conflicts and irritations still existed, but détente continued. There may literally have been "no love lost" between Ralph and Shirley Newton, but by now neither had any more need for the other. Ralph Newton's remarriage was successful, and Shirley Newton was about to graduate cum laude and cum fiancé, a man she loved and whom the children liked as "a very special friend." With everyone's self-respect in working order, there was no longer any need for scapegoats.

A problem for many single parents who still have children at home is how to enjoy an adequate social life without incurring the resentment of their children. It's not so much the single parent's dating that is hard for the child to deal with as it is the parent's discomfort, evasiveness, or irritability with the child's questions and complaints.

Single parents cannot protect children from such distress by pretending they do not date—not when the children see or hear them when they leave or enter the house, when they overhear phone calls, sense pleasurable anticipation, or see the parent "dressed up." Any such evasion would deny the children an honest sense of what it's like to be adult, and any "protection" it might afford would reflect only adult insecurity. Nor is it any more satisfactory to let children come along on dates, to reassure them that they come first. How inappropriate and dull for kids to be dragged along to adult activities in which they have little interest. Such extremes are, of course, rather ludicrous when seen objectively. Not at all ludicrous is a parent's concern about children being confused when they see their mother or father date different people, some once, some many times. But at least we can acknowledge the confusion and persuade children that such dating is one way to get to know someone well enough to discover whether the person will become a casual friend, a special friend, or someone we love.

When that someone we love becomes a lover, additional concerns arise. If the sexual side of the relationship takes place outside the home, with the children unexposed and uninvolved, then no explanation is necessary—*if* there is also no change in the children's routine (for example, the parent is home when the children wake up in the morning). If, however, lovemaking takes place in the home, children *are* involved, and acknowledgment and explanations are both desirable and necessary. We may prefer to believe our children are unaware of what is going on because they are too young, or we assume they are asleep, but even very young children are sensitive to changes of attitude and routine. Children are readily aroused at night by unfamiliar sounds—a bedroom door being locked, water running at two A.M., the clink of ice cubes, the hum of a new voice. Certainly if the lover stays overnight and is present in the morning, children will be aware something is different.

At such times, what children think and feel about the situation is governed largely by the reaction and attitude of the parent. The more comfortable the parent generally feels about his or her sexuality as a natural part of life, the more comfortable children will be. If we respond openly to children's questions and comments, they will accept our intimacy with another adult, as they would other adult activities. But if we respond to "What is he [she] doing here?" with a guilty "Go back to sleep!" or "It's none of your business!" or an evasive "He [she] just came over to lend me a book" (at midnight or seven in the morning?), the children will pick up our evasion and discomfort and be burdened by it. If, even more destructively, we respond with a lie—"No, you didn't hear anyone. It must have been a dream"—we put children in the position of being forced to doubt their own perceptions. Given a straight, simple answer—"Yes, Joe [Joanna] was here last night" or "Joe [Joanna] is staying over tonight"—children can accept their own perceptions and their parents' behavior.

While children should not be directly involved in the specifics or details of their parents' sexuality, it is appropriate for them to know that sexual intercourse is one way adults have to express how much they care about one another, that it is a private, personal, and rather wonderful part of being grown up, just as they already understand that staying up late, driving a car, pursuing a career, or deciding on a vacation are all parts of the pleasures and responsibilities of being an adult. What an adult can acknowledge comfortably, a child can accept and use as a building block for healthy growth and development.

The Helene Bower who sat facing me was not the same woman I first met eight years before, when she and her husband were getting divorced. At that time it was almost impossible to see how lovely she was under her thick makeup, or appreciate how bright she was under her façade of baby-doll helplessness. Mrs. Bower had originally sought help for Chet, age six, and Melanie, age two, shortly after her husband left following the death of their third child nine days after his birth. The baby had been microcephalic and Mr. Bower was unable to bear either his own horror and grief or his wife's. Though he was very close to Chet and "adored" Melanie, he immediately sought a job transfer and moved several hundred miles away. Despite the distance between them and the infrequency of visits (usually monthly), he managed to maintain a fond "absent father" relationship with his children. He never was willing to see me, so all my original work was with Mrs. Bower, Chet, and Melanie. It had been difficult work, for the three of them had been doubly bereft, but it had been effective and for the past seven years Helene Bower had grown from a dependent "doll" into a mature, successful, and admirably functioning woman. Having started a working career as a clerk-typist, she had been steadily promoted to her present position as office manager in a large firm. With her flawless skin and huge eyes undisguised by Pan-Cake makeup, she was also strikingly attractive. Melanie had emerged as a talented little girl, "crazy about" horses, art, and gymnastics. Chet was a "natural athlete," active in intramural sports, and a "science nut." Both kids were doing well in school, had good peer relationships, and when last seen appeared to be thoroughly healthy. I wondered what was going on, what was the "problem" Mrs. Bower referred to when she required an "emergency appointment."

Ms. Bower, as she now preferred to be called, filled me in quickly. Over the years she had dated several men, but none seriously, and few she had introduced to her children. Chet and Melanie knew she dated. They expressed curiosity, and she responded comfortably and appropriately— "Mostly," she added, "because I never really got deeply involved, so it was easy to be casual." Now, however, things were different. She had been dating one man for six months and he wanted to marry her. She wanted to marry him. She had introduced Perry to her children, and both of them liked him, although Chet had made it clear, "I only like him as a person. I don't want him as a father. I don't want my life to change." Melanie, on the other hand, was pressing her mother to marry Perry, even while complaining bitterly whenever they went out in the evening. In fact both children were resenting her going out so much—"You're never around anymore!"—and to make matters worse, Chet had begun making snide innuendos like, "You certainly don't play backgammon when you visit Perry's apartment," while Melanie would get giggly and silly. "I really don't know what to tell them other than that I'm an adult and responsible for my own conduct. Perry has asked me to go away for a weekend with him next week and I really want to go, but I don't know what to say to Chet. And I certainly don't know how to tell him I want to marry Perry when he feels so strongly about it. On the other hand, I'm not about to throw away these years until the children are ready to leave home."

I agreed and pointed out that Chet should not, in turn, be made to feel responsible for her throwing away those years. "For all his protests it would be frightening for him to believe he can control your life. At fourteen he's neither mature nor experienced enough to make adult decisions. But he is old enough to be highly aware of, and not yet comfortable with, his own sexual feelings, making him all the more interested in and jealous of your sexuality. He must be experiencing all sorts of mixed feelings. He's jealous of the time you spend with Perry, he's probably worried about the changes which will occur when you marry Perry, he's certain to feel a loyalty conflict about Perry taking his father's place, and he's reluctant to give up his role as the only male in the house. He needs to know he's *entitled* to all those feelings, just as he needs to know that you are entitled to your feelings."

"I have no intention of encouraging Perry to be Chet's father, nor does Perry ever assume that role. The strange thing is that Chet and Perry really do like each other, and Perry is comfortable hearing Chet talk about his father. He never tries to take over. That's all in Chet's head."

"Then he needs to be helped to see that, as he needs to be prepared for any realistic changes in his life, and he needs to know the difference between fearing something and having something really happen. He was willing to talk with me before, and now I think would be a good time for me to see him again. He may want you to sit in, but if he's very angry at you, or very frightened, he may wish to see me alone. I prefer you come too, but let's let that be his decision. By the way, when Chet embarrasses you about Perry or tries to make you feel guilty, you must get very angry at him.''

"Angry! He infuriates me! And I know he gets me so upset because I'm uncertain in my own mind. Most of the time I think I'm adult, responsible, sensible, liberated. The kids have turned out well, I enjoy my work, and I like myself. Then this comes up and I suddenly feel like a helpless kid. Chet picks this up and hits me with it. If I didn't feel so stupidly guilty, Chet couldn't get to me.''

"Ms. Bower, if you know all that then you really don't need me to make any interpretations. Once you realize what's going on, you have a choice of how you are going to deal with it. Let's think about what *you* want, because the better you feel about yourself and your decisions, the more easily Chet will be able to adapt to your decisions.''

We talked, just the two of us, for several sessions. Ms. Bower was able to understand that old inner conflicts about her worthiness, desirability, and sexuality had been reexcited by both Perry's wish to marry her and Chet's jealousy and anger. She was also able to see how much she had matured and to know that she was no longer either helpless or functionally dependent upon outside approval. By the time she came in with Chet, much of her "guilt" had disappeared, because she no longer needed to feel guilty.

Chet, on the other hand, entered my office as he must enter a football game—prepared to attack. "Look, Mrs. Kliman, you know I call you when *I've* got a problem, but this is *her* problem. It's just not fair! I've told my mother exactly where I stand. I don't need another father. I don't want my life to change. I won't move, and if she has to run around acting like a whore, well, that's her problem!''

"Like a what, Chet?"

"Oh, you know what I mean."

"Chet, I'm not even sure *you* know what you mean."

"Ah, come on! I mean like when she goes to Perry's apartment and screws around. I mean, *she's my mother!* And I don't like her to act cheap."

"You've certainly been doing a lot of thinking about this, Chet. I wonder, do you think Perry 'acts cheap'?"

"No, but he's a man. That's different."

"I see. You're saying if a man 'screws around' with a woman that's okay, but if a woman 'screws around' with a man that's cheap. You spoke of 'not fair' before—I wonder if your assessment of 'screwing around' and cheapness is fair. Aren't you making a lot of assumptions that are not only 'not fair,' but also not true?"

"Like what?"

"Like assuming that Perry is being shoved down your throat as your father, instead of seeing him as your mother's future husband. Like worrying about moving when no one has such a plan. Like being concerned that your life is going to change in some terrible or overwhelming way. Chet, you've got many powerful feelings about all of this—and you're entitled to feel any way you wish. But it does seem you're hurting yourself more than you have to. Maybe one problem is your worry that you'll lose your mother to Perry. Is that what you really think?"

"Naw, not really, it's just Mom spends so much time with him now and she's not around as much as she used to be. But no, she's a pretty good mother." He grinned a bit sheepishly.

Ms. Bower grinned back not at all sheepishly. "And you're a pretty good kid, Chet."

"Your mom tells me she thinks you and Perry have a good friendship going. What do you think? What do you like about him?"

"Mostly that he's easy to talk to, and he's got a good

sense of humor. And he's as much of a science nut as I am. He's a science writer and he knows what I'm talking about. He's great as a friend. I just don't want him as my father.''

"Chet, you *have* a father, and no one can or wants to take his place. You describe Perry as someone you like and who's interested in you. Do you think this will change if he marries your mom?''

"If he's around all the time it would have to. I mean, if my best friend moved in I'm sure we'd argue more than we do now.''

"Would that be so terrible? Can't good friends disagree or argue and still be good friends? Maybe you're remembering the arguments your father and mother had when they split up, and that worries you. Only it's not the same. You are no longer a little boy, you're a teenager with the capacity to discuss and solve problems instead of just being scared by them. Your mom isn't the same way she was eight years ago either—adults grow too. And Perry is not the same man your father was.''

Chet conceded that I might be right. "Only I still feel funny about the whole thing. It sounds stupid, but I do. I mean, if they did get married they'd both be around a lot more. It's weird—I'm out a lot, at school, at sports, at my friends, even on weekends, so I don't really need Mom, but I kinda like to know she's there. Boy, that's dumb!''

"No, Chet, it's part of being an adolescent. Some of the time you're independent and off on your own, and some of the time you want your mom to take care of you. You're testing new experiences, changing and growing physically, intellectually, socially, emotionally. You're reconsidering many things you used to take for granted. When so much is changing inside you, is it any wonder you want to keep what's outside stable and certain? It's a tough time for you, and for everyone who cares about you.''

"You said it.''

"Okay, now you can say it too. You can talk thoughtfully about what concerns you, rather than waste your time and energy on attacks.''

With that, Chet turned to his mother. ''Mom, you know I'm going to Boston with Tommy and his parents next weekend, and Melanie's going to visit Grandma, so you can do whatever you want—only I don't want to know about it and I don't think you should tell Lanie if you're going away.''

Ms. Bower shook her head. ''Chet, I've no intention of discussing the weekend with either of you except to leave a number where I can be reached in an emergency, and to say I'm spending it with Perry. I have nothing to hide or be ashamed of. I will listen to what you say, and respect your feelings, but I will continue to follow my own judgment.''

''Okay, Mom, okay, you don't have to come on so strong! Tell Lanie whatever you want—it won't matter anyway, she's so goofy about Perry already.''

''I may be coming on strong, Chet, but you still have missed the point. I'm not asking for your permission! I will make my own decisions about myself and for my children. I won't ignore your feelings, and I'll try not to hurt them, but neither will I be bound by your ideas on child raising, for both our sakes.''

''Okay, Mom, okay, point taken. Is our time up? I'm starved!''

The next several months were reruns of the exchange in my office. Chet remained somewhat uncomfortable through the courtship and after his mother married Perry and Perry moved in with them. But he did not come to feel hassled in the way he had feared. Helene Bower, now Helene Randall, felt secure enough to maintain a balance of firmness and affection with Chet. Perry Randall was sensitive enough to ''ride along'' with Chet and rarely let himself fall into the traps Chet set for him. In time, Chet was able to say to his mother, ''You can say 'I told you so'—I like having him around.''

Melanie had few problems in dealing with her mother's remarriage. She started calling Perry "Step," saying she couldn't call him "Daddy" and didn't want to call him "Perry" but she did want a "special name" for him. He accepted his nickname as it was offered, with warmth and affection.

Problems will occur and recur for the Randalls over the next several years, but given their essential maturity and sensitivity they should be able to cope with them. The Randalls have been fortunate in that they neither avoided nor ignored the problems that lead to faulty or destructive relationships in one-parent dating and eventual remarriage. The children had years to become accustomed to their mother's dating (longer than was necessary for them to adapt, though not longer than their mother needed to find a man "right" for her). During this time Helene Bower did not overexpose her children to a series of men around whom they could build disappointing fantasies. The few "dates" she introduced her children to she introduced appropriately. After Chet and Lanie met Perry, she arranged for all their joint activities to be child-oriented—times that could be enjoyed by all. She never referred to Perry as "your new father," so she didn't burden the children with loyalty conflicts. That Chet experienced such conflict on his own was acknowledged, and Chet eventually was helped to discriminate between his fears and reality. He was also helped to feel less conflicted about his sexual feelings, to accept them as part of natural growth. As his mother became more comfortable in her sexual relationship with Perry, Chet felt less compelled to act judgmentally in his assumed fantasized role of lover, husband, and father. His "acceptance" of female equality was demonstrated when he painted a large EX on his favorite T-shirt, a shirt that had read MALE CHAUVINIST PIG.

Of course not all single parents remarry, whether for neurotic reasons or well-thought-out and adaptive considerations. While an intact family may be the ideal, it isn't the only family constellation that can nurture healthy children. As is stressed throughout this book, the better the parent feels about himself or herself, the better the child will feel. Whatever a parent can cope with, a child can be helped to cope with. Countless healthy children are being raised in one-parent families. What determines the well-being of a one-parent family more than anything else is if the parent has selected singleness out of considered choice, rather than from fear or hatred. Parents who are single by choice have the interest and energy to invest in their own, and their children's, worthiness. They also have the sense of security necessary to utilize the "extended family" (relatives or friends) to mitigate the lonely feelings so common in single-parent families. But however adequately they function, single parents continue to be burdened by the attitudes of society. Married people, be they neighbors, judges, or therapists, can feel threatened by the recently singled and respond out of prejudiced fear rather than individual assessment. As the death of a friend forces us to face our own mortality, so dissolution of a marriage makes us face our own marital vulnerability. Subliminally threatened, we either fight (criticize or condemn) or flee (withdraw from a preexisting friendship). At the risk of being judgmental myself, I suggest that such a prejudiced loss is a loss to us all.

For children, the influence of modeling is not to be underestimated. It is particularly crucial in such situational crises as separation, divorce, and reattachment. Children hear what we tell them, and they also see what we do and how we react. It's confusing to children (and adults) when we stress the importance of respect and politeness and then act disrespectfully and impolitely. Of course none of us can always behave in exemplary ways, but all of us can respect ourselves and our children enough to explain or apologize when our behavior is inappropriate, unreasonable, or hurtful.

Such consideration enhances our self-understanding, and through it we can effectively teach our children to understand themselves—and eventually others. Building blocks of self-awareness—they are essential if we are to avoid the trap of projecting our worst fears of abandonment upon others subconsciously chosen to enact those fears. We are all subject to "fate," but we are also able in large part to influence and shape our destinies—as well as those of our children.

Violation

6

Rape is violence. Our society assumes it to be an act of passion and sexuality, but the rapist's intention is to degrade violently, to humiliate, hurt, and terrorize his victim. Throughout history rape has been deemed the right of conquerors, as with swords, crossbows, cannons, or flamethrowers they killed the vanquished men and violated their women. In some countries today custom and law declare a raped woman to be unclean in one sense or another—a used vessel unfit to lie with a decent man or to bear his children. In our country we have no such social customs or laws, but we have tended, until very recently, to see the raped woman as tainted, even infected with the evil of her rapist. Rarely did a rape victim dare to report she had been raped, lest the police, or a physician, neighbor, or relative react as if it had been her fault—as if she had been "asking for it." (The recent ruling of Judge Simonson in Wisconsin is a case in point.) The female victim of an ordinary mugging is not asked why she was walking alone, why she is wearing a sweater, why she uses makeup; but a rape victim is. Sadly and outrageously, the result of such prejudiced attitudes is that the rape victim is revictimized by the very people whom she believed to be her care-givers and protectors.

In my own community, as one fortunate example among many, there has been over the past half-decade a systematic effort to revise local laws (for example, an eyewitness corroboration is no longer required to prove rape), to reeducate those involved in direct service to the rape victim (police, emergency-room personnel, schools, lawyers), and to offer a county-wide network of support for the victim. Similar "rape clinics" and "rape squads"—specially trained groups of police usually attached to the county sheriff's office—have been and are being organized all over the United States. With women less afraid to report rape, and from a careful, nonjudgmental evaluation of the data, we have learned a great deal about the crime. We know that women who are raped are not usually young and beautiful, nor do they dress or act in a seductive manner. Simultaneously we have learned more about the rapist. He does not look like a fiend, he looks like an ordinary man. He may or may not be married, may or may not have children, may or may not be an otherwise stable and productive member of the community. He is a man who both hates and fears women and who derives his sense of manhood and worth by humiliating women. He is vicious, terrifying, and sick.

Ellie Mack was just seventeen when I first met her. Unlike most rape victims she did not come to see me through referral by the Rape Squad, by a physician, social agency, or her family. She came alone and secretly. She knew she needed help but was so ashamed of what had happened she had not told her parents, much less the police or her doctor. When I asked her how she had known about the Center, she reminded me I had run a workshop at her high school the previous year under the title "Rape: A Crime of Violence Against a Revictimized Victim." She told me how scared and ashamed she felt, and since I had talked about those feelings at her school she hoped I would understand. I told her I was glad she'd had the courage to see me and added, "I hope you also have the courage to tell me exactly what happened, and then we can work out together how you can best be helped."

Ellie had gone out the night before to visit a girl friend several blocks from her home to study for a history exam. She had left her house at seven-thirty, telling her parents that she would be home around eleven. Her going was not unusual—she and her friend Dena often studied together. But when she arrived at Dena's she was told that her friend had a virus and felt too sick to study. Ellie got back on her bike and started to return home. As she rounded the corner a car pulled out suddenly and sideswiped her bike. Ellie fell, the car stopped, and a man got out and ran to her. He seemed altogether solicitous and apologetic. Other than a scraped elbow and knee Ellie was unhurt, but the bike was a mess and couldn't be ridden. The man insisted on taking her home. He told her he would pay for the repair of the bike and that he wanted to tell her parents that the accident was entirely his responsibility.

Ellie started to cry. "I know I shouldn't talk to strangers or take rides from anyone I don't know, but this was different. I mean, it all made such sense and he seemed so nice. The wheel was all bent and I couldn't have carried the bike and my books up the hill to my house. I just thought he was a decent person. But when we got to my street and I told him to turn right up the hill, he continued straight ahead. I told him he had missed the turn, but he didn't say anything and kept driving. I got a bit scared and asked him to turn around and take me home. He grinned at me and told me to keep quiet and he wouldn't hurt me. I really got frightened then. I started to cry and scream, and then he pulled a gun and told me to shut up or he'd kill me. I couldn't stop crying and he hit me with the butt of the gun just above my knee." She pulled up the leg of her slacks and showed me a huge bruise with the skin split. Still crying, but now softly, she told me that he took her to some woods on the edge of town. Holding the gun on her, he ordered her to get out of the car very slowly and walk in front of him.

"When we were deep in the woods, he told me to take off my clothes, but I was so scared I couldn't move. He raised the gun and shot over my head. I thought someone must have heard the shot and I started to run. He grabbed me and slapped me and said, 'I told you if you were quiet I wouldn't hurt you, but if you make noise or try to get away I will kill you. Now do as you're told. Take off your clothes!' I just kept whispering, 'Please, please.' And then it was weird. He said if I couldn't do it myself he would—and he did, but he didn't tear them off; he took them off very carefully and folded them neatly on the ground! I was scared out of my mind, but even then I thought it was crazy. He kept smiling and told me to keep very quiet and to kiss his feet. He had pushed me down so I was kneeling in front of him. He was all dressed, but his fly was open, and he was holding the gun so it was right next to—right next to his penis—and then he threw me backward and he raped me. It hurt, it really hurt, he just jammed it into me, and I began to cry again. Only this time he just smiled and said, *'Now* you can cry.' He jammed so hard I was bleeding, and when he stood up he was still smiling and pointing the gun. He said, 'Oh, I got me a baby bitch! You just keep quiet. I know where you live, and if you talk I'll come back again, baby bitch. Maybe I'll come back anyhow.' Oh, God, what am I going to do?"

Ellie and I talked for a long time. She could describe the rapist very well and had a fairly good description of his car. I told her she needed the help of a physician, the police, and her parents. I stressed she had been hurt and abused, but she had not made any of this happen, any more than if she had been mugged or robbed. We spoke practically about her medical and psychological needs. I told her I knew a physician who could help her body heal and make sure that she wouldn't develop any venereal disease or become pregnant, a doctor who had helped many rape victims and who would be very gentle. We then spoke about her parents and why she was so afraid to talk to them. She described them as loving and caring, but she was afraid they'd be angry that she hadn't fought more, and for not telling them right away. I said it would have been very foolish to fight anyone with a gun, and gently I wondered with her if perhaps she wasn't blaming herself for not fighting back, and then projecting this sense of blame onto her parents. We decided that needed more thinking about and talking out, but right now our first step was to contact her parents so that they could care for her. She agreed to let me take her home and talk with her parents in her presence.

At first Mr. and Mrs. Mack were indeed angry with Ellie for not telling them immediately, but then they were overwhelmed by rage at the rapist, and became loving and supportive of Ellie. Within the next few hours Ellie was treated by a physician and had met with the Rape Squad. With her parents' and my support, she was able to see that reporting the rape had been her right and responsibility. She also came to see it as a facilitation of her psychological healing, moving her as it did from a passive and humiliated position into one of constructive action. She gave an excellent, full description of the rapist and helped the police artist draw a picture of him. She was also able to remember the color, make, and style of his car, as well as the first two numbers of the license plate. It took weeks, but the rapist was found, arrested, and brought to trial.

By that time I had worked intensively with Ellie, individually and with her family. She was able to integrate the experience as one of violence, to understand that the rapist had used his penis as a weapon as he had used his gun. She was able to accept that she had not been made love to, but had been assaulted. She was even able to understand the quality of excitement that had accompanied, but in no way dominated, her other feelings of fear, humiliation, and rage. Such excitement is usually stimulated in the victims of all aggressive acts, and an experienced rape counselor knows the importance of helping rape victims understand that it is one of the many expectable reactions to attack and is just as "normal" as fear.

Ellie's parents fully cooperated in the family work, talking openly and proudly, outside the family as well as within, about how courageously and honestly Ellie had coped with the rape experience. The freedom with which Ellie was able to talk gave impetus to her high school principal's request to organize another rape seminar in which Ellie would lead the discussion and I would act as consultant. On the day Ellie testified at the rapist's trial, the courtroom was crowded with her family, neighbors, and schoolmates, male and female. She had gone from helpless victim to master of her own private and public self in nine hard, painful weeks.

I see Ellie now on follow-up once a year. She is in college and is undecided as to whether she is more interested in social work or marketing research. She is continuing to grow well as a healthy young woman who has mastered a potentially pathogenic life experience.

Ellie had a lot of help to cope so well. She lived in a community that was already sensitized to the psychology of rape, a community that had developed an entire network of individuals, agencies, and institutions ready and able to offer appropriate service and support, and she had a family who loved her—no less than before her violation. We as individuals cannot demand that parents love and understand their children as sympathetically as did Mr. and Mrs. Mack, but we can demand that our communities develop services for the victims of *all* violent crimes, rape included. Until we make such demands and they are met, Ellie's recovery will continue to be the exception rather than the rule.

Mildred Kahn was referred to me by her gynecologist. "She's a sixty-eight-year-old widow who lives alone," he told me on the phone. "Two days ago a man posing as a telephone repairman got into her apartment, knocked her unconscious, and raped her. Other than a mild concussion and some vaginal abrasions, she is physically unharmed. In fact, she's in excellent shape. She appears to be handling the experience well, but since she has no family in the area I thought it would be helpful for her to see you. You could do an evaluation and perhaps give her a chance to talk." I told him to have her call me and I would see her immediately.

Mrs. Kahn came in the next morning. She looked me over very carefully, sat down, smoothed her skirt, and said, "What's a nice girl like you doing in a job like this?" I deadpanned, "What's a nice girl like you doing getting victimized like this?" We both laughed. "Okay," she said, "I call you a girl, you call me a girl, neither of us are girls so we can talk. But I can't tell you much. He said he was the repairman, I let him in, started to show him the phone in the kitchen, and as I turned around he hit me and that's all I remember until I woke up. So now I have a headache, my jaw and tongue feel on fire, and I hurt down there, but I have four children and six grandchildren so sex is no big deal. I'm glad I was unconscious, because I probably would have tried to protect myself and maybe he would have killed me. He hurt me enough when I didn't do anything! So what can I tell you. I'm no young girl, I have no honor to lose—that went out with steel corsets—I can't get pregnant, and after the penicillin I won't even get a social disease. So it happened and I live with it. I saw worse in my lifetime. So what's to talk about?"

"Mrs. Kahn, you're one tough lady, but tough or not

you have been assaulted. We're not talking about sex, we're talking about violence. If you got hit on the head and your purse was snatched, wouldn't you have feelings about it? Wouldn't you be angry, outraged, frightened? I would! I'd be frightened to find that my own home wasn't safe, I'd be furious that I was abused, and I'd be talking with the police demanding protection and that they find the rapist. Are my feelings so different from yours?''

She looked away from me. ''So maybe the feelings aren't so different. But I wouldn't want the children to know—God knows, not my grandchildren! What would they think of me, their Nana, treated like a slut. God forbid. Sure I'm scared. I already got a new lock and a one-way mirror installed in my door. I'll never let anyone in without checking with the phone or gas or whatever company first. And I'm angry, so what? What do I do? Go beat up somebody? You get all filled up with anger and hurt so it stays inside and maybe the headache hurts longer and you just feel helpless. That's the worst. Oh, that's the worst. I'm old, but not so old I'm ready to be helpless. I still play cards once a week with my friends. I still work. Yes, sixty-eight, I still work. I teach needlepoint. I even go out. Nothing exciting, just an old friend—but dinner, a movie, even sometimes a play, it's nice with an old friend. My kids tell me I should marry Harry, but if you know someone for forty-six years as a friend, that's what he is, a friend, not a husband.''

''Forty-six years is a long friendship. Does he know you were raped?''

''God in heaven! No! He's two years older than I am. You think I want to shock him to death?''

''Maybe he'd be more shocked that such an old friend couldn't turn to him when she needed him. Maybe he'd be more shocked that his old dear friend was letting herself be helpless when she didn't have to. Maybe he'd be hurt and angry that you shut him out.''

''So many maybes. Funny, you talk like my mother

used to, and I'm old enough to be your mother. She called it *sechel*, you know what I mean? Common sense. What do you call it?''

"I'll call it anything you wish. But it is common sense if we feel helpless to do something active to help ourselves, to get someone else to help us do it. And it's common sense to let a friend be a friend. If Harry needed a tender arm around him, wouldn't you want to be there? To offer that arm?

"But I don't just talk, Mrs. Kahn, I also listen. You saw the man who attacked you. You do needlepoint so your eyes must be good, and you probably have a talent for detail. You could describe him to the police. You have the energy and interest to work, date, play cards—take that energy and look at mug shots, and if that doesn't work, describe him to the police artist. Perhaps his method of getting into your apartment is known to the police. You could assist them, and with some work and luck they might catch him and stop him from raping someone else. And if you at least tried, would you still feel so helpless?"

"Maybe not, maybe so. But all right, I'll talk to the police, but only if they promise no name in the papers."

"I think they can promise that. And I think they'll be grateful for all the help you can give them."

"All the help I can give them! I help someone, I don't feel helpless. Common sense! Okay, done! Now, you think you have to see me anymore?"

"What do you think, Mrs. Kahn?"

"I think, maybe, one more time after I see the police. To let you know if it works or not."

"Good, let's set up a time now for next week, and if you want to talk to me before then just give me a call."

Mrs. Kahn did work with the police, and her eye for detail proved a great help. She made a positive identification of the rapist, even noting a small triangular scar on his right wrist that she'd seen when he held up his fake repairman's

I.D. card. I saw her that one more time. She was feeling better, her physical injuries were fully healed, and her psychological injuries were healing by her active involvement in detecting and identifying the rapist—as well as by her zest for life, work, and friendship.

Such brief intervention is not unusual in cases where the rapist's victim is adult, mature, and rejects the victimized status. To cope with this crisis, just the latest in a long life, she needed only a "nudge," as she put it. It would add a bit to my sense of professional dignity to have it called "intervention," but as I told her, I'll call it anything she wishes.

Working with Liz Lawson was an entirely different experience. Liz was barely eight years old—too young physically, intellectually, emotionally, and socially to understand what had happened. That Liz had been overwhelmed became dreadfully clear when Mrs. Lawson told me Liz had been abducted, beaten, choked, and raped the evening before but could remember nothing between getting into the car and arriving at home some five hours later. Mrs. Lawson told me that Liz's physical injuries were very painful, but not critical or permanent. However, the pediatrician had strongly recommended that Liz see me because I was "someone who knows how to help children who have something awful happen to them, and knows how to help them with their worries." Although no one in the family had had any experience with therapy, Liz's parents were determined to "do anything to help her." Eleanor Lawson's voice broke as she told me, "Liz was such an elfin child; she was the laughter in our home, so bubbly with her funny grin and mischievous, big brown eyes. Now she just huddles close to me and doesn't say a word." I told Mrs. Lawson that Liz had been badly shocked but I believed we could work together to help her become her elfin self again. We made an appointment for four-thirty that afternoon.

Liz looked awful. She clung to her father's arm and walked into my office with the rigid movements of a robot. One of her eyes was blackened, swollen, and nearly shut; there was a long, bandaged cut running down one side of her mouth and there were dark bruises on her throat. The only part of her that still seemed to be the Liz Mrs. Lawson had described to me was her bright red hair, a mass of short, bouncy curls. Liz sat down gingerly in the chair. I knew it wasn't just fear or shyness, she must hurt like hell! She looked at me quickly, then looked at her mother. I introduced myself and asked Liz what she understood about coming to see me. Her voice was hoarse and low, probably as a result of having been choked. She said she knew I helped children who had been hurt, and with tears running down her face she added, "And I was very, very hurt, I was—was—Mommy, what's the word, I forget." I said, "Often when something very scary happens we don't want to think about it because it makes us feel so bad. Then we try hard to forget it." Eleanor Lawson stroked her daughter's arm. "Liz, honey, the word you forgot is rape." "But Mommy, I don't remember that. I don't remember being hurt at all. I just know it hurts now." I nodded. "Liz, maybe you can tell us just what you do remember."

Liz got off her chair and cuddled in her mother's arms. Then she looked at me. "I was skating at the pond after school. I always do that when the ice is thick and the sign says it's okay. Lots of my friends were there too, but then they all left to go home and I decided that I wanted to practice my figure eights. I don't do them very good yet. Then a car stopped and a man yelled at me to get off the ice. He told me I shouldn't be there after five and it was against the law and he was a policeman. I got scared 'cause I didn't know it was against the law so I got off the ice, took off my skates, and started to walk up the hill. He stopped and showed me his badge. He told me he would have to take me home and tell

my parents what I had done and they would have to take me
to the police station. I was scared but Mommy always told
me to go to a policeman if I was in trouble. I got in the car
and that's all I remember until I got home. I was bleeding all
over and I threw up on the steps. Then Mommy grabbed me
and took me to the hospital. Dr. Marcus was there. Oh, it
was awful. I don't want to talk about it anymore!''

"Liz, you don't have to talk about it anymore now.
Perhaps there's something else you'd like to do. There are
lots of toys and crayons and games in this room.''

Liz went to the bookshelf and took down the box of
crayons, a pen, and some blank paper. "I love to draw. I'll
draw a picture.''

While Liz was drawing, her parents filled in some details. (Liz told her mother it was all right if she or Daddy
talked. "I just want to draw.'') Mrs. Lawson said she began
to get worried when Liz didn't return home at five-thirty. She
knew Liz was skating, but Liz always came home before
dark. "I sent my husband down to the pond to see if Liz was
still there, and then started calling all of Liz's friends. But no
one had seen her since four-thirty. By then it was after six
and we both were terrified. I called the police. One of the
detectives went to the pond and came back with Liz's transis-
tor radio and I wanted to die. I knew something terrible had
happened. Liz carried that radio with her everywhere, even
to school. I thought she had been kidnapped, but we don't
have any money, so that didn't make sense. The police were
searching everywhere but they didn't have a clue. None of
the neighbors had seen Liz or the man or the car. It was a
nightmare. Then, just before ten, Liz appeared on the front
steps. She was vomiting and there was blood on her face and
her jeans were torn and soaked through with blood. I must
have screamed . . . I don't remember either. But I did ask my
sister to call the detectives so they could take my husband to
meet us at the hospital. Liz just kept crying and crying. Dr.

Marcus was very gentle, but finally he had to give her a shot to quiet her down. She was pretty badly torn inside and her face was cut. Dr. Marcus said it was a knife cut, but he used butterflies so Liz wouldn't be scared by the stitches. He was the one who told Liz she had been raped. I don't think he should have, but as he put it, Liz's body was already telling her that she had been hurt and she needed to know what happened, especially since she couldn't remember. He called it a traumatic amnesia.''

Liz handed me her drawing and asked if I would pin it up on the cork wall with the other drawings I had there. I told her I would after she told me a story about the drawing. It showed a forest, a clearing, and a tiny animal hiding at the root of a big tree. Liz proceeded to give me a remarkably graphic description of her rape couched in the symbolic images of her drawing. She said, "This is a little animal who lives in a hole. One day she goes out of the hole and a big animal comes. At first he isn't such a big animal, he's sorta like a big dog, but then he's a great big animal like a bear and he tells the little animal that he wants to live in her hole. The little animal cries and says, 'Please don't take my hole away. I won't have anyplace to live.' The big animal gets mad and hits the little animal with his claws and then he jumps into the hole. The little animal is crying and the big animal comes out of the hole and tells her it's his hole now and then he goes in and out of the hole over and over until the little animal runs away and hides. And that's the end of the story. Now will you put it on the wall?''

I pinned Liz's picture on the wall and told her she had given me a very important story that really helped me to understand how worried and scared and hurt that little animal was. I said, "Little animals can be really terrified when a big strange animal changes size, and hurts and forces a little animal to do things she doesn't want to do.'' Liz nodded and Mrs. Lawson began to cry. I acknowledged to Liz that Mommy understood the story too and was feeling very sad for the little animal, and for her little girl who had been so terrified and hurt too. Liz came very close to me and said she had a secret. I replied, "I'd like to hear your secret, but this is a good place to share secrets with *all* the people who love and care about you." Liz whispered loudly enough for all to hear, "I can't make pee-pee. I want to, but it hurts too much."

Mr. Lawson put Liz on his lap. "Baby, do you remember Dr. Marcus told you that it would hurt for a few days until you are all healed inside. Remember he gave Mommy medicine to soothe the hurt?" Liz got off her father's lap and turned to me. "Am I going to come back again and draw?"

"Liz, I would like it very much if you came back. Do you want to?"

"Yes, I like to draw."

Over the next six weeks I saw Liz and her family together many times. In the first week Liz developed new and very understandable symptoms. She began to withhold her bowel movements as she had her urine. She frequently had screaming nightmares, but could be comforted by her parents. She began to eat less and less, until she only took juices. She needed a night-light and refused to have her bedroom door closed. And finally, she refused to let her mother out of her sight.

Liz, her parents, and I worked on all of this. Liz was helped to understand that withholding her urine and feces was caused partly by the pain she'd had for the first few days after the rape, but was also her way of controlling, together with her not eating, what entered and went out of her body. The pediatrician wisely refused to prescribe an enema because that would have been another "rape," and on the tenth day after the attack she proudly told me she'd had a huge bowel movement. She was helped to remember her nightmares (all of them as symbolic of the rape as had been her picture-story that first visit) and to make connections between the little animal and herself, between the big animal and the rapist. As the drawings and nightmares were interpreted she began to remember more and more. She began to draw pictures of herself and the rapist, rather than of animals. Eventually the drawings and her accompanying verbal descriptions helped her pick out a photograph of the rapist from the police files. The detectives were marvelous. They allowed me to keep the copies of the mug shots so that I could integrate the questioning with the therapy and not have Liz subjected to even the gentlest grilling.

In the first week of therapy I was brought to realize there was more to Liz's reluctance to eat than just a manifestation of controlling what was put in her body. She asked me one day what belly buttons were for. I asked her what she thought, and she responded, "That's where babies come out of their mommy's tummies." I said that was an idea lots of children had and asked her how she thought babies got into their mommy's tummies. Liz said with great seriousness, "I think mommies eat a lot of food and that makes the babies."

I told her that lots of children thought that too. "But I think your Mommy can explain the real way babies get in their mommy's tummies, and what the belly button really is." (It would have been easy for me to do the explaining, but it is not the role of the therapist to take over parental function, and it is most helpful if children learn the facts of life from their parents. Surprisingly, in this age of sex education, a great many parents, even in what might be considered more enlightened social populations, do not reveal the facts of sex to their children until they are approaching puberty.)

Mrs. Lawson began to laugh and said, "Lizzie, when I was your age I thought almost the same thing, but let me tell you what really happens." And she did, warmly, lovingly, and clearly.

This was the turning point in Liz's treatment. Now Liz could eat, urinate, defecate, play, and live freely. She had gone through a brutalizing rape, but with the help that she got from her parents, the police, her friends, and her brief crisis intervention therapy, Liz emerged not unscathed, but healthy and strong. She is now twelve, she has retained her elfin quality, she has grown well, and she was very proud to report to me last month in our yearly follow-up, "I just got my first period and it didn't hurt at all!"

Taking a look at what happened and what didn't happen to Liz should give us some guidelines to assist and facilitate the healthy growth and development of child rape victims. Her parents, despite their terror, treated her as an assaulted child and got her immediate physical care from a sensitive, aware pediatrician. At no time did they, the physician, the police, or the neighbors, assign blame to her, for indeed she had done nothing wrong. Her family was able to bear the pain of listening to their child recover her memory of the violent attack, and shared their appropriate reactions (fear, rage, tears, love) without embarrassment or restraint. While they did not always agree with either the pediatrician's or my initial recommendations, they listened and usually put them into action. Mrs. Lawson was particularly intuitive to and supportive of Liz in explaining sexual matters and making a clear distinction between lovemaking and rape. The detectives were able to put Liz's welfare before their own job requirements and cooperated fully in having me serve in their place with Liz. Her parents and I were thoughtful about Liz's temporary symptoms and allowed her psychological healing time without pushing or demanding that she remember, stop clinging, or start eating, though there were many frustrating times for us all. And finally, the entire network in which the Lawsons lived rallied support and care: there were no whispers or shunning.

Such a climate may be rare or difficult to create, but it is possible.

It is not only women who are raped. So are infants, boys, and young men.

The rape of a male is no less an act of violence than is the rape of a female, but our society tends to respond to the rape of a male with even more horror, and with greater defensive determination to revictimize the rape victim. From my own area, it appears no coincidence that over the past two years not one of a dozen reportedly raped boys, representing various social, economic, religious, and racial groups, and from the entire county of Westchester, was allowed to complete even a brief course of interventive treatment; only one boy was allowed the advantage of mastering the violence imposed upon him. In my experience the parents are unable to bear the shame, disgust, and horror of having their son talk about the attack; they even punish him for talking about "such dirty things." No matter whether they believe the child, their tolerance for their son's fear, excitement, helplessness, and pain is so low, they usually move to another community or state rather than stay and help the boy heal psychologically.

When Wilma Arnold returned home from work one afternoon, she found her five-year-old son, Ricky, in tears. The baby-sitter, a seventeen-year-old neighborhood boy, told Mrs. Arnold that Ricky had been teasing the baby all afternoon and he had punished him by refusing to let him watch TV. Mrs. Arnold had little patience for Ricky's misbehavior and told him to go to his room until dinnertime. The sitter left and Ricky began pleading with his mother to listen to him. Still annoyed, she told Ricky to sit quietly while she made dinner. Tearfully he told his mother the sitter had threatened to kill Ty, his baby brother, unless Ricky took off all his clothes and let him play with his "pee-pee." Mrs. Arnold had known and trusted the sitter for six months, so she became angry and slapped Ricky for making up such a nasty story. Ricky couldn't stop crying or talking. He told his mother the sitter had hit him with a belt until Ricky let him sit on top of him and push his "pee-pee" into Ricky's mouth, and then he woke up Ty, took off his diaper, and pushed his penis into Ty's bottom. Enraged, Mrs. Arnold spanked Ricky for being such a "nasty, disgusting, lying" child. Ricky fled from the room screaming, "Go see Ty, he's all bloody!" Frightened now, Mrs. Arnold went in to see nine-month-old Ty. He was lying on his side whimpering, his face wet with tears, his diaper and sheet covered with blood.

Stunned and disbelieving, she grabbed the baby and yelled for Ricky to come with her to the doctor. Dr. Mendez examined Ty carefully and confirmed he had been raped, that he was suffering from severe rectal lacerations that would need surgical repair, and urged Mrs. Arnold to contact the police immediately while he arranged for Ty's hospitalization. He then examined Ricky, and apart from the strap welts on his buttocks and legs (Mrs. Arnold had spanked him with her bare hand and could not have made such marks), he pronounced Ricky physically fine, though he warned Mrs. Arnold that her older son had been badly hurt psychologically. He told her the Center staff was experienced in helping raped children and she should call us immediately. Mrs. Arnold refused, saying she didn't want anyone to know. Dr. Mendez told her he was bound by law and ethics to report the rape and gently suggested it would be easier for her and Ricky if she and he filed the report together. He again urged her to make an appointment for Ricky and herself at the Center, adding that she had been hurt by what had happened to her children and she also needed help in dealing with her own feelings and Ricky's.

Overwhelmed, exhausted, and frightened, Mrs. Arnold agreed to call me after Ty's surgery. And she did, two days later. We spoke for half an hour. She refused to come in to see me, or to bring Ricky. No matter how I tried to help her understand that she and Ricky had been victimized, that he deserved, as well as needed, psychological assistance, she refused to make an appointment. Rather she informed me she couldn't face her neighbors or co-workers ever again. She was planning to move out-of-state the following day! I acknowledged that was one choice open to her, but moving away wouldn't remove the terrible experience to which she and her sons had been subjected. She was adamant. She would leave tomorrow. I told Mrs. Arnold I hoped she would think about what Dr. Mendez and I suggested and added I would be glad to recommend an experienced therapist or clinic in the area to which she was moving. She refused to divulge her destination. "No one is ever going to know. We'll start with a clean slate." She hung up.

Had this been one of my first experiences with raped boys, I would have attributed the failure to my inexperience. Perhaps I could have handled the phone call more skillfully, but it was clear that Mrs. Arnold was in too isolated a condition to utilize the network of support that was available to her. Abandoned by her husband some seven months before, she was already feeling rejected and less than desirable. Never an outgoing person, she had made no reliable friends at work and had little time to cultivate neighbors. Her "extended family" was scattered and out of touch. It can be surmised that she harbored some resentment, conscious or unconscious, against her sons, who in many ways reminded her of her lost husband. Previously an adequate if not ideally affectionate mother, she was too bereft of her own sense of self-esteem, and perhaps too guilty about her lack of empathy for her sons, to continue mothering them appropriately. I have no follow-up on this family, only a sense of sadness and frustration.

The Arnold case serves as a singularly stark example of the resistance that characterizes parental reactions to homosexual rape. Usually we are able to see raped boys and their families for several sessions before the parents prematurely abort the intervention. Occasionally three or four sessions are adequate to facilitate the boy's active mastery of the assault, but only if the parents are strong enough to act as therapeutic allies and help the child continue the work at home. Even when the intervention is interrupted too soon, the initial sessions serve to sensitize both parents and child to the task at hand. A model has been set up that can be followed. It is all right—it is important—to express any and all of the feelings associated with the rape. *Nothing* emotionally felt is bad, nasty, or dirty. Even very young children can be aided in understanding that they have been violated, and that the person who raped them is sick. Most importantly, children need help in knowing that their own sexual feelings are healthy and appropriate, that they cannot seduce healthy adults into raping them, and that such violent acts of aggression are the responsibility of the rapist alone.

Closely allied to rape, especially in its effects on children, is incest. Although the majority of incestuous relationships are not violent, they do sorely burden children, especially young adolescents, with serious confusions about their own sexuality. Once thought to be the custom of "primitive," uneducated, or deprived families, incest is now known to cross every social, religious, racial, economic, and educational level. It happens in the nicest families! And it can become a model for life. Mother-son incest appears to be rare, and there is little in the literature about it. Brother-sister incest is less rare, but I have had no experience working with such siblings. Father-daughter incest is the most common, and here my experience is considerable.

Rona Barker was seven when she was referred to me by the Department of Social Services. The department's dossier on the Barker family was thick, and I knew a great deal about Rona, her fourteen-year-old sister, Rhoda, and her parents, Rudy and Emma Barker, before I met any of them. Mr. Barker was a "pillar of the community." He held a managerial position in a large corporation, was a faithful churchgoer and a member of the church's board of governors, belonged to several service organizations, and was "liked and admired by everyone." Mrs. Barker, described as a small, immaculately neat, rather depressed woman, was irregularly active in the church's auxiliary, the P.T.A., and the local hospital volunteer bureau. She was generally regarded to be "a bit sickly, but very nice and a hard worker when able to work." Rhoda had until recently been an honor student, was a member of the girl's intramural hockey team, and was a dedicated Girl Scout. Rona was described by her teacher as a very bright child, but inattentive and disruptive with her flirty, clingy manner. On the surface, the Barkers hardly appeared to be a family that would be involved with Social Services and the County Court, or be the object of community outrage.

It was unfortunate that during the two weeks that elapsed between the discovery of the family's incestuous practices and the referral for situational crisis intervention, shocked, vengeful wrath descended upon the Barkers. Mr. Barker had been jailed, Rhoda had been moved out and was living with the family of a girl friend, Mrs. Barker had fractured her ankle and was "confined to bed," and everyone was arguing about "the fitness of Mrs. Emma Barker to retain legal guardianship of her daughters," with strong recommendations to make the girls wards of the county and place them in foster care. Crisis intervention was long overdue.

The incest became publicly known in a way that was sad but not unusual. One evening when Mrs. Barker was attending a meeting, Rhoda returned home from Scouts earlier than expected and found her father in bed with Rona. Enraged, for she believed herself "to be the only one," she ran to her room, locked her door, and called the police. Rhoda had been having intercourse with her father since she was six. Now she found herself displaced by her baby sister. As is not uncommon with incestuous fathers, Mr. Barker preferred the young undeveloped body of Rona to the now sexually matured body of his teenage daughter.

I never had an opportunity to work with Mr. Barker.

When it became clear that I would be working with Mrs. Barker and the girls, Mr. Barker refused to see me "on advice of counsel," despite my statement that any session with me would be privileged.

It took considerable effort to convince Mrs. Barker, Rhoda, and Rona to come together to see me, but they finally did. Emma Barker hobbled on crutches into my office and took the chair closest to mine. Rhoda pulled her chair as far away from the others as the small office would permit. She plunked down, crossed her arms over her chest, and stared angrily at me. Rona huddled in the chair next to her mother's, her head down, her hands tightly clasped between her thighs. I looked at this isolated group for an instant and said, "I wanted to see you together because what has happened involves all of you, together as well as individually. I am very sorry I was unable to arrange for Mr. Barker to be here too so that your whole family could have the chance to deal with what is, what has been, happening."

Rhoda said through clenched teeth, "Then I wouldn't have come. I never want to see him again. I hate his fucking guts!"

Mrs. Barker protested furiously, "Rhoda, don't you dare talk that way. That's filthy and I won't stand for it!"

"Who the hell do you think you are, dear Mother, to tell me what you'll stand for! Where the hell were you when I tried to tell you what I was standing for? Ha, I mean what I was lying down for! You wouldn't listen! You never listen. At least he used to listen to me. He always used to listen." She began to cry.

Tearfully, Mrs. Barker whispered, "But I didn't know. I didn't know. I couldn't believe it. I just couldn't!"

Rona hadn't moved all this time, but tears were coursing down her face and wet patches were beginning to form on her skirt.

I acknowledged what I saw. "I see, despite what each of you has or hasn't said, that you all are sharing something right now. You are all crying. I'm glad you can share that, and in time, as you get to know me better, you may let me help you share other things, too." Startled, each looked at the others, then turned back to me. I continued, "Rona, you are the only one who hasn't said anything. I can see that you are sad and scared, maybe you can help me understand more of what you are feeling and thinking."

Again Rona put her head down. "I don't know. I didn't think it was bad. I mean, it wasn't like they said. Daddy never hurt me or scared me or anything like they tried to make me say. We just played games. It was nice. He'd make me all tickly and I'd tickle him and then he'd squirt. That was funny! The only time he got mad was when he came in the bathroom and I was playing in the tub with Elmer's glue and he asked what I was doing. I said I was pretending to be him. He wasn't really mad, but he told me not to do that because Mommy or Rho might come in and they'd get upset. He said it was our secret. And I never said anything. They kept making me say bad things about Daddy, but I wouldn't. It's not true, he never hurt me, we just played the tickle game." She began to cry again. "I miss Daddy, why can't Daddy come home?"

Rhoda and Emma Barker were no longer crying; they were listening, their faces drained to an ashen pallor. Mrs. Barker reached for Rona, who almost leapt into her lap. Rocking and crooning, her mother told Rona not to cry. "I'm not mad at you, Baby, I'm really not mad. I'm just sorry, so sorry, Baby. Don't cry, don't cry. Everything will be all right."

Rhoda sat rocking herself. "It used to be like that with me. He never hurt or threatened me. I was so angry and jealous I told them he did, but he didn't. I was so jealous I wanted to hurt him, to punish him, but it wasn't true. Oh, dear God! I'm so ashamed. Everybody's making me feel so filthy."

I shook my head. "Rhoda, there's nothing filthy about you or Rona. All little children have tickly sexy feelings. That's part of being a human being. And all little girls would like to play such 'games' with their fathers. But it is a father's responsibility to help his daughters grow and develop healthy, age-appropriate sexuality. It is not a father's right to seduce his daughters. Your father has some serious problems, which interfered with the way he parented both of you. He has a kind of sickness that made him use you both, and even though he used you gently and without threat, he did burden you in ways you were too young to handle. Your father can get help with his problems much the same way you are now getting help."

Rhoda interrupted, "But he's in jail, and I sent him there. He can't get help in jail. Would it help if I tell them it wasn't true that he forced me or hurt me?"

"I'm quite sure it would help a great deal, Rhoda. But it's going to be a hard thing to do. You're only fourteen—you're not all grown up—and you're going to need your own help so that you can grow up and feel good about yourself. You tell me that you feel guilty, angry, abandoned, and hurt. Those are hard feelings to live with alone. My work is to help people cope with what has happened to them *and* how they feel about what has happened. I also think you and your mother need each other very much right now. You need an opportunity to be her daughter rather than her rival, and she needs an opportunity to be an involved mother to you, rather than a passive accomplice."

Mrs. Barker turned toward Rhoda. "Rho, I didn't know because I couldn't let myself know. I failed you. I failed everyone. Please, please forgive me. Let me try again, come home and let me try."

"I'll talk with you, Mom, but I'm not ready to come home. Maybe in a while, not yet."

Mrs. Barker nodded her head and cradled Rona more

tightly in her lap. Rhoda came over and knelt in front of Rona. "Baby, I'm sorry I was so mad at you. You weren't bad. It wasn't your fault. I'm not mad at you anymore. Friends?"

Rona nodded. "You really scared me, Rho. Promise you won't get mad like that anymore?"

"I promise, Baby. Friends?"

"If you don't call me 'Baby'!"

"Okay, no more 'Baby.' We'll be friends again."

She playfully mussed Rona's hair and Mrs. Barker put her hand on Rhoda's.

Again I acknowledged what I saw. "Now the three of you are sharing gentleness and understanding. I'm glad you can share different kinds of feelings. I think we've all done good hard work today. I'd like to see each of you again this week, this time individually. Then next Monday I'd like to see you again together." They all nodded and we set appointment times.

Later that day Rhoda went to the police and told them the truth. I had consultations with the district attorney, Social Services, Mr. Barker's lawyer, and the police. With each I shared my impression that the children, the community, and the Barkers would be better served if Mr. Barker entered intensive therapy to help him deal with his illness, rather than be kept in jail. I strongly recommended that Mrs. Barker not lose custody of her children, and I committed myself and them to a three-month minimum of family and individual therapy. My recommendation included that an Order of Protection preventing Mr. Barker from seeing his children *not* be issued, rather that frequent supervised visits be set up so the children would be given a direct chance to deal with their father and their feelings toward him.

With more rapidity than is usual in such cases, my recommendations were accepted, probably because they were identical to those of the psychiatrist who evaluated Mr.

Barker. The court put Mr. Barker on probation with the demand that he see his psychiatrist four times weekly for as long as the psychiatrist deemed necessary.

I saw Rhoda, Rona, and Emma Barker individually once a week and as a family group once a week. My work with all three was supportive, educational, and interpretive. Mrs. Barker was aided in facing the marital and sexual problems that contributed to her collusive, passive, "unknowing" partnership in the incest. She was helped to be a more active, involved mother to both her daughters and worked hard in regaining their trust. After three months she spontaneously said she felt she needed more long-term individual treatment to overcome her "sexual problems" (really the symptoms that blanketed her fragile sense of herself). She accepted referral into analytically oriented psychotherapy.

Rhoda had stated her problems clearly in our initial session, but she also needed help in giving up her father as her primary sexual love object, to refind herself as a young adolescent, to give up her precociously overstimulating and burdensome sexual behavior, and to allow her parents to parent her appropriately.

Rona, although developmentally more vulnerable than Rhoda, was less damaged. While greatly overstimulated by the mutual masturbation with her father, she had not yet had an adult genital experience; she had never had intercourse. She did have many problems of guilt, feeling it was "all my fault" (expectable for a child in the developmental stage of magical thinking), and she missed her father. Yet she needed support to know it was all right for her to love him even though he had a "sickness."

By the end of the three months of intervention, both girls were considerably improved in their relationships. I began seeing them only in the family group weekly, and after six months I saw them monthly. Now, three years later, the entire family is living together. Mr. and Mrs. Barker, still in their own treatment, are relating more appropriately as husband and wife, and as mother and father. Rona, now ten, is a well-functioning child who relates happily to her friends, does well in school, and no longer is disruptive, seductive, or clinging. Rhoda, in her last year of high school, is again an honor student and is ambitious to become a lawyer. She has a few close girl friends, and one boyfriend, two years older, whom she has dated for the past year. Rhoda's sexuality has reemerged on a healthy peer level, and despite some residual conflict in finding her lover "not the same as Dad," she is able to give and derive sexual pleasure. She is aware of her father's lingering hold and reluctantly joked with me about her lover. "Being two years older than me isn't enough to make him a father figure, is it?"

Despite how well Rhoda and Rona are currently doing, I am not satisfied that sufficient time has elasped to be sure they will continue to grow without developing sexual problems. Rhoda has not succumbed either to frigidity or promiscuity, symptoms that commonly plague girls who have had a sexual relationship with their fathers. (Frigidity can be a defense against the guilt that accompanies incestuous sexual pleasure, and promiscuity can be the frantic, unending search to find someone "who loved me as much as Daddy, who's as good as Daddy.") I will continue to see Rhoda and Rona on follow-up for many years. Indeed, I would like to continue seeing each into marriage—until they have a daughter reach the age of six, the age they both were when their father began his incestuous relationships with them.

The story of the Barker family is less unusual than most of us would like to believe. It challenges many of our assumptions: incest does not occur in "good families," incest is always the result of threat or rape, the incestuous parent is a thoroughly bad person, girls who are seduced by their fathers are permanently damaged, mothers are innocent and noncollusive in the father-daughter incestuous relationship.

Large-scale studies of incestuous families indicate that when psychological intervention occurs the children tend to do quite well and are able to resume their lives in appropriate ways. Their parents, however, appear to do less well, probably because the incest is usually a symptom of severe, long-term psychological pathology.

The seducer in incestuous relationships between parent and child is not always the parent. A father once came to me at the Center deeply troubled by his having had sex with his fifteen-year-old daughter two nights before, at her prompting. As I listened to this tormented man's account of what had happened, I realized that the case was not appropriate for crisis intervention—its cause was an external event that had occurred four years before; it was a long-term problem, in other words, and rather than take it on myself I referred him and his daughter to a therapist for long-term treatment. It remains, however, an extraordinary and significant example from my experience of the profoundness of latent sexuality between father and daughter.

The precipitating event four years before was the family's desertion by the mother. "She just took off," the father said. "No note, no explanation, nothing." (Almost unheard of not many years ago, maternal desertions are becoming more and more common, perhaps a distortion of the New Feminism.) The daughter had always been closer to her father, and under pressure of overcoming the mother's loss they drew closer still. His work required traveling much of the time, and now when he came home his eleven-year-old daughter, having been left with cousins or at a friend's house, would welcome him back effusively. Complaining of nightmares in his absence, of being scared and lonely, she began to sleep with him. "It was a big bed," the father explained, "and she would give me a big hug and then curl up in a tight little ball. I never really thought anything about it." Sometimes, when school vacations allowed, he would take her along with him on his trips, always sharing the same room, and always she would join him in bed.

The daughter's rapid physical development over the next few years did nothing to inhibit their intimacy, certainly not on her side. She would run around the house in bra and panties, or a sheer nightie, and her father, though uncomfortable with her growing attractiveness, decided not to make an issue of her behavior, not at the risk of being called "an old fogy."

When his daughter's spring vacation coincided with a ten-day trip he had to take, they went off together. "The trouble started almost immediately," he related. "I'd be falling asleep and she would start stroking the back of my neck. I told her to cut it out and let me get my rest. Another night I woke up and she was spooning behind me. It was a shock, but I thought it was my dirty mind so I got up and moved to the twin bed. I tried to talk to her about it the next day, but she was so light and gay I didn't want to spoil it. Then two nights ago I thought I was dreaming and I sort of half woke up and I had an erection and she was lying on top of me. God help me, I screwed her. It was crazy, I knew it was her and I didn't. I half thought it was my wife come back. I did know I was crazy with excitement and so was she. When it was over and I realized, really fully realized what happened, I couldn't believe it. I tried to talk to her, to tell her I was sorry, but she turned over, curled up into a little ball and fell asleep. Curled up, she was my little girl again."

The "trouble" had, of course, not started on this trip, but four years earlier with the mother's desertion. The event left both father and daughter feeling lonely and abandoned, and was a severe blow to their self-esteem. Moreover, the daughter now had to move from childhood to adolescence without a mother or consistent mother-substitute to identify with, and to keep a parental perspective on her relationship with a father to whom she had, most naturally, felt "closer" even when the family was intact. Unconsciously she sought to take her mother's place—partly to fill the void left in her own life, partly to fill the void left for her father—and the further she developed physically, the more she had physically to fulfill that role of wife. Yet behind her motivation lay a most common impulse—adolescent girls, subliminally recalling how adorable and seductive they were at the Oedipal age of four, revive passionate feelings for their fathers with physical maturation. Her problem, however, was not that impulse but a four-year situation that erupted into action, just as the father's problem was not in feeling a response to his daughter's natural and seductive attractions, but his inability to resist them.

As is often the case with fathers who allow their adolescent daughters to seduce them, he was a heavy drinker—the problem had increased reactive to the loss of his wife—and the fuzziness of his reactions during the actual intercourse bespoke not only the effects of alcohol, but the deep need accrued from his four-year loss. For both father and daughter, the "seduction" was less an aberrant physical action than the inevitable climax to a long-term psychological dysfunction, which was why their case lay beyond my resources to treat, beyond situational crisis intervention. I had been drawn into it four years after the real crisis. Four years too late.

While it is rare for children to be the deliberate seducer in an incestuous relationship, even when they are it remains the parental responsibility to distinguish between child and adult sexuality. Parents who allow a six-year-old or a fourteen-year-old to seduce them are often otherwise "good parents"—they would never, for example, allow such a child to drive a car before he or she is of legal age.

There is probably no one factor alone that predisposes a family to incest. There are, however, a number of variables that place families at high risk. Among them are: parents who themselves were engaged in incestuous relationships as children; parents enmeshed in immature and ungratifying relationships with their spouses and who turn first for affection and then for sexual love to their children; alcoholic and drug-addicted parents; isolated or abandoned parents who, fearful of adult relationships, turn to their more naïve and less demanding child; and parents whose impulse control is fragile and who are hypersensitive to the natural sexuality of children. The incestuous seduction of children is usually a slow process, comparable to adult "courtship," but invariably it proves burdensome, disruptive, and guilt-provoking for all involved.

Most of us who have worked with incestuous families are convinced that punitive action resulting in removing the child from the family only serves to compound the psychological damage already done to the child or adolescent. If the responsible adults are willing to engage themselves in therapy, individually and in family group sessions, it is possible for the family to reconstitute itself healthily. The child can be relieved of guilt, the father (in the case of father-daughter relationships) can be rehabilitated, and the mother can mature sufficiently so that she no longer needs to be a silent partner. It works out of a natural process—once a pathological family balance is no longer comfortable for family members, there is an active seeking for a new, more tolerable, and healthier balance.

I am not entirely comfortable writing about rape and incest in the same chapter, for as I emphasized at the start rape is an act of violence, not sex, while incest can be an act of seduction. What is common to both is the use and abuse of the human body; both excite feelings of guilt and shame in the victim, and often the victimizer; and both have the potential of eliciting such passionate and vengeful reactions in communities and individuals that the victim is revictimized while the victimizer is punished but not treated. We respond to both, especially incest, as we used to respond to leprosy. Our own aggressive, sexual, sadistic, or guilty impulses are stimulated and frightened by the intensity of our feelings, and are projected onto others as deserving harshness. We used to beat, chain, and jail schizophrenics, and none were helped, much less cured. We may be subtler today, but until the abuse of sexuality and the combination of sexuality and violent aggression are recognized as an illness, as schizophrenia is now, we will remain unable to diminish their frequency or cure the sufferers.

Death
by Design

7

Suicide is death by design. That is the only statement I can make about it without qualification, for the complexities of suicidal motivations and reactions are so profound as to leave all generalities open to argument. Except for military and rescue operations in which electing to die is deemed heroic, suicide has been viewed in our society as shameful, so shameful that families, clergy, police, and physicians often attempt to keep the manner of such deaths hidden and speak rather of "accidents."

Increasing attention has been paid to the phenomenon of suicide over the past several years. Dozens of studies conducted by physicians, therapists, sociologists, and federal agencies have made us aware of suicide as a major public health issue. We have learned that a large proportion of automobile accidents are disguised suicides, and that suicide is rapidly on the increase among adolescents. We have learned, but find it most difficult to believe, that children between three and twelve deliberately consider and do commit suicide. And we have learned that suicide, like child abuse and alcoholism, tends to be passed down to the next generation, not via the genes but by unconscious identification with the willfully abandoning parent.

The method of suicide can tell us a great deal about the dead person's motives. Violent and self-mutilating suicides (jumping from heights, shooting through the head, slashing wrists, and so forth) clearly demonstrate both rage turned inward toward the self and rage turned outward toward survivors. The discovery of such disfigured, bloody bodies is horrifying. Self-hanging usually reflects the victim's wish to be punished—and to punish. Self-immolation is a violent statement of rage, helplessness, and a demand to excite guilt in others. Drug overdoses, or combinations of pills and alcohol, are perhaps the "gentlest" method of suicide, but may be made violent by accusatory notes left to family, colleagues, or friends. One-vehicle "accidents" often combine ambivalent feelings of anger (in the mutilation of the body) and protectiveness (it will seem an accident; insurance will be paid) toward the family. A suicide involving two or more vehicles expresses literal murderous rage.

Whether or not any person has the "right" to commit suicide is a question that has been debated over the centuries by theologians, legislators, therapists, sociologists, and philosophers. I have no answer for anyone but myself. I can imagine that in circumstances such as loss of brain function, chronic and unrelievable severe pain, or total isolation, I would wish to die and would design my own death. Such real situations would be intolerable for me, and I believe I would have the right to make a decision to end them for myself. I would never try to impose that belief on anyone else.

All of us who have worked with people who express suicidal ideas have learned to *take them seriously,* and to assess carefully the profundity and intensity of the idea. Suicidal ideas may be manipulative, neurotic, psychotic, reactive, or realistic. Such despairing comments as "I can't go on'' or "I wish I were dead" indicate a person at risk who is pleading for help. These people cannot be helped by "That's ridiculous!" "Don't talk like that!" "Look at all you have to live for," or, most damaging of all, by ignoring their plea. Potential suicides at highest risk are those who not only say they wish to die, but also have a plan worked out. Often we can assist such people to find other less drastic and irrevocable alternatives; sometimes we cannot.

It is true that people who are determined to die will find a way despite the most intensive care, tight restraints, and careful observation. Except for disaster survivors and the bereaved—people in a reactive depression appropriate and expectable following an acute loss (and as such frequently accessible to brief intervention that facilitates mourning)—I have had little experience with people who threaten or attempt suicide. I have had considerable experience working with the families of people who have committed suicide. Without exception, the surviving spouse, children, and parents react with pervasive guilt, conscious and unconscious, which makes them particularly vulnerable to expiatory acts of self-punishment including accidents, illnesses, and breakdowns in family relationships.

Mrs. Lois Roberts phoned me less than eighteen hours after learning that her husband, Curt, had killed himself by jumping off a bridge onto the pavement sixty feet below. Stunned and horrified, she had only one question: "What can I tell the boys? They're babies, Ned is two and a half and Kevin is only four. I can't tell them what their father did, I can't. But what *can* I tell them?"

I asked, "Can you tell me how you learned of your husband's suicide, and what the children have been told?"

"I haven't been able to tell them anything. When I came home yesterday afternoon I found the boys eating Popsicles in the living room. It was so close to dinnertime that I was annoyed and went into the kitchen to ask Patsy, the sitter, why she let them eat so close to dinner. Patsy just looked at me and burst into tears. She couldn't stop crying as she told me the police just phoned and said my husband was dead. I must have screamed, and then it was crazy. The doorbell rang and it was two policemen. I told the boys to go upstairs, told Patsy to call my parents and Curt's brother, and asked the police what happened. They told me, but I didn't believe them. It had to be a mistake. He was fine when he left in the morning. They told me there was no mistake. I can't remember what happened then, but suddenly the house was full of people. My parents, more police, neighbors, my sister. Everybody was talking and crying. I didn't believe it was true till someone gave me Curt's wallet and his class ring. Someone must have called my doctor because suddenly he was there and he wanted to give me a shot, but I wouldn't take it. I yelled at him to leave me alone, I yelled at everyone to get out, but more and more people came. When I went to check the boys, they were already put to bed. Kevin asked me why everyone was here and where his daddy was. I told him to go to sleep and I'd talk to him in the morning. What am I going to do?''

"Mrs. Roberts, I can see how terribly difficult this is for you and how you want to protect the children. But from what you tell me Ned and Kevin already know something awful has happened. They know their daddy didn't come home, they know you are desperately upset, they know the house is full of people and everyone is acting differently than usual. It isn't possible that the boys did not overhear the talking, the crying, the shouting. How much and what they have overhead we must find out so we can help them cope with the loss of their father. If we don't share the reality of their loss, they are going to have to deal with it all alone, and they are much too young to do that without your help. The best way for you to help them is to tell them directly that their daddy let a terrible accident happen to him and he is dead. And that is why you are so upset. They need to know *why* you are so upset, and to know that it's appropriate for you to cry and yell, and that *it is not their fault*. It's going to be hard for them to understand all you say, and they will not react the way grown-ups do. Despite all the pressures on you right now, I hope you will talk to the boys today. Each hour they have to struggle alone only makes it more difficult for them. I want you to come *with the boys* to see me this afternoon so I can help you help them."

Mrs. Roberts protested that there were so many arrangements to make she couldn't bring the boys to see me that day. I allowed that there must be many pressing matters, but suggested that her first priority was to help her sons and herself cope with the next few days. She agreed, and we talked briefly about how she would tell Kevin and Ned that they were coming to see someone who understood the kinds of worries little children have when their daddy has died. Lois Robert said she would do her best.

A few hours later, Ned entered my playroom clinging tightly to his mother. His brother Kevin looked quickly around the room and went straight for the game shelf. He took down a game of checkers, spread the board on the table, and said, "Ned, come play checkers with me."

Mrs. Roberts responded, "Kevin, you can't play checkers, and neither can Ned."

Kevin insisted, "I can so play." As he set up the board somewhat haphazardly, Ned jumped off his mother's lap and began to climb onto a small bench. He immediately fell off and began to whimper. When his mother tried to comfort him he broke out of her grasp and climbed on top of a small table and jumped off, this time landing squarely on his feet. Mrs. Roberts started to scold Ned for his behavior, but undaunted, he climbed up to a large chair, wriggled around on its broad arm, and again fell to the floor. This time he banged his elbow and really cried. Mrs. Roberts picked him up saying, "I told you to stop jumping around. Now come sit by me!" While Ned was jumping and falling, Kevin was engrossed in his game. Holding one checker, he was methodically jumping each man on the board, over and over again saying, "Now I will jump you, and you, and you, and you. . . ."

I acknowledged what I was seeing. "Kevin, I see you are playing a jumping game and I think you must be having lots of thoughts about checker men jumping. Ned is younger than you are and doesn't know how to play with checkers, but he's showing us his thoughts by jumping and falling himself." Without interrupting his game, Kevin said to me, "My daddy's dead. He had a 'assident' and he's dead. He won't come home ever! That's right, isn't it, Mommy?"

Ned ran over and hit Kevin. "You're bad! You're a bad boy!"

Lois Roberts began to cry.

I said, "Your mommy is crying because she is so sad. You're right, Kevin, your daddy let a bad accident happen to him and he is dead and he can't come home ever. That's scary and that's why Ned hit you and called you bad. He's mad and scared. He doesn't really understand what's happened, or even what 'dead' means. But both of you have heard a lot of talk about falling and jumping and Daddy being dead. It's so hard to understand, but you can't stop thinking about it. That's why I'm glad your mommy brought you here so we can talk together about Daddy being dead and your scary thoughts and worries."

Mrs. Roberts was rocking Ned in her arms. "I can't believe they heard so much."

Suddenly Kevin said, "The guinea pig at school got dead. The cage got open and it fell out and got squished. Then it didn't move."

"I guess, Kevin, that as awful as it was to see the guinea pig 'get dead,' it's easier to talk about than Daddy getting dead. But maybe you could try, and maybe you could tell us what's worrying you now. I bet you have lots of questions and worries.''

Kevin came over and sat next to me. ''What's going to happen to Daddy now?''

I looked at Lois Roberts. ''I think it would help Kevin if you could answer him and tell him what to expect at the funeral. The children will need to be with you then, and it will help them if they take an active part in the ceremony. Even a very brief part would be of value.''

She took a deep breath. ''I didn't think it would be good, but maybe . . . only everyone will be so upset, I thought it would be better. . . .''

''The children already know everyone is upset. With their daddy dead they need more than ever to be with you and the rest of the family. They need to experience everyone else's grief so they can learn to handle their own. They need to see people cry or be angry, and to discover that it's safe.''

Mrs. Roberts pulled Kevin toward her. Ned was snuggled on her lap. ''Honey, Daddy will be put in a coffin, that's a big box, and then he will be buried in the cemetery. We will all go to church and then we'll go to the cemetery and watch them put Daddy's coffin in the ground, and we'll say a prayer and then we'll all come home.''

''But then Daddy can't breathe!''

I agreed, ''You're right, Kevin. Daddy won't breathe. Remember you told me the guinea pig didn't move when it was dead. When animals or people die they don't move or breathe, or eat, or play, or work, or go to the bathroom, or cry, or laugh, or feel anything anymore. That's what being dead means, it means that all the things we used to do in life we don't need to do, and can't do anymore.''

''Not feel *anything*?''

''No, Kevin, not feel anything.''

Ned had wriggled out of his mother's lap. He was listening quietly and sucking his thumb. "Mommy, I hungry. I want cookies."

I said, "It's been a long, hard session and I'm sure Ned is tired and hungry. I think he is also telling us that he has an empty lonely feeling in his tummy and wants to fill it up." I walked with them to the door. I asked Mrs. Roberts to call me in the evening so we could discuss some additional things that might make the next twenty-four hours a bit easier. We also set up an appointment for the next afternoon. As Kevin left he paused a moment and asked if I were really sure his father couldn't feel anything at all, even "mad." I told him I was very sure, but suggested that his question was very important and we would talk about it more next time.

I had learned a great deal during the session. It has never ceased to surprise and gratify me how clearly preschool children communicate through their actions and play. Ned's falling and jumping and Kevin's checkers jumping game were such obvious messages, they were impossible to miss. Even their mother saw and understood the connection.

I was aware of several areas for concern. In enacting what he heard, Ned was not only trying to master what he could not yet understand, he was also making himself more vulnerable to injury. I would share this concern with Mrs. Roberts and would suggest that extra precautions be taken to insure his safety. I would also share the fact that she and Kevin, though able to comprehend more, were also survivors and thus themselves more susceptible to injury.

Kevin's last question was a blockbuster. Out of all the possible ways of feeling, Kevin expressed concern about anger. At four he was an Oedipal child, developmentally at a stage in which he passionately loved his mother and fiercely resented his father. But he also loved and needed his father, even to protect him from his own wishes. Now that his father had died Kevin had an Oedipal victory, a victory he was too young to handle. Moreover, he was also in the developmental stage of magical thinking, and would imagine it was his anger and resentment at his father that had caused his death. In asking about his father feeling "mad," Kevin had been telling me he was afraid of both his father's retaliatory anger and the power of his own anger toward his father.

Both children would be apt to behave more clingingly toward their mother, being afraid of losing her too. And she, also lonely and frightened, would be tempted to encourage clinging—probably allowing them to sleep with her, a frequent practice of bereaved parents, but one that is too stimulating for young children. When young boys sleep with their mothers in their father's absence, especially if the father has recently died, they feel they are taking their father's place. Daddy always slept with Mommy, now Daddy is gone so I will sleep with Mommy. While ostensibly just protecting young children from their lonely, frightened feelings, the surviving parents gives tacit approval and agreement to the fantasy that the boy can replace the man. It is far more supportive and helpful to sit with the young child until he falls asleep in his own room. On the other hand, the common practice of allowing children to jump into bed with a parent (or parents) in the morning to read the comics together, or have a pillow fight, or just cuddle is not overwhelming for children. There is no fantasy of replacing a parent; it is an affectionate, happy time.

I was also concerned about Mrs. Roberts. She would need an opportunity to vent and explore her own anger, helplessness, and guilt. I would have to see her individually as well as in family sessions to allow her the chance to cope with her adult problems. She would need a great deal of support over the next few months, including parent counseling to understand how out of phase children and adults can be in accomplishing the work of mourning, and to assist her in selecting the most growth-promoting ways to help her sons adjust to the loss of their father. I expected a most difficult several months for the family—and for me.

And they were! Guilt and rage were the predominant themes of our sessions. After an initial period of shock followed by dramatic overidealization of her husband, Lois Roberts began to express her anger. "How could he do this to me!" "How could he leave me with two babies!" "Didn't he know what he was doing to us!" "I hate him, I hate him, I *hate him*!" While able to express such "unacceptable" feelings in individual sessions with me, she had little tolerance for Kevin's anger, either expressed directly at his father ("He was a mean Daddy") or projected onto his family and friends (Grandpa was "mean" when he wouldn't give Kevin extra money; Ned was a "stupid doody-head" when he touched Kevin's truck; the kids at nursery school were stinkers and wouldn't play with him). Gradually Mrs. Roberts began to accept her own anger as appropriate and thus found it less frightening. This enabled her to become more empathetic and supportive of Kevin and his anger. She moved from "Don't you dare say that!" to "I see you're very angry, Kevin. I understand that, I've been angry at Daddy, too, and then took it out on you." Then she would listen to his angry words, comfort him, and help redirect his energies into something less threatening, such as "beating up" his punching bag, or hammering his peg set, or even a pillow fight.

She also became more immediately responsive to Kevin's statements of guilt. When he shared with us the belief that his father had killed himself because he, Kevin, was a bad boy (he left his toys around, fought with Ned, and called his father a "bad name"—all things that had irritated his father), Mrs. Roberts was immediately supportive. She told him children are too little to make grown-ups *do* anything—what grown-ups do is their own responsibility. She explained many times that his daddy killed himself because he had a kind of sickness that wouldn't let him think clearly, and he couldn't get help for his sickness because he wouldn't tell anyone about it.

This, indeed, turned out to be the truth. In reviewing the

several years that preceded her husband's suicide, Mrs. Roberts and I discovered there were many times in which her husband had sent out disguised or openly depressed messages. Although highly successful in his work, he frequently expressed disappointment in himself, his creativity, and a supposed lack of appreciation from his colleagues. He'd say, "Oh, hell! Life's just not worth it!" but he would appear to recover quickly and involve himself in his work, his family, and his friends. Upon reflection, Mrs. Roberts realized that over the past six months her husband had been unusually irritable with her and the children, but she had felt his annoyance was justified—a household with two children under five is rarely tranquil. Then she recalled a number of arguments he had had with friends at parties; they would start out as friendly discussions, but he would rapidly become angry and abusive. She recalled trying to talk to him about this, only to have him retreat into silence. She also reported he had been having difficulties sleeping—he could fall asleep easily, but would wake up in the middle of the night and not be able to go back to sleep. About the same time he gained thirty pounds. She told me she had pushed him to see a doctor about his sleeping difficulty and his weight, but he would get angry and tell her, "Go mother the boys, not me!" With all of this there were many times he was loving with her and the children—as he had been the morning of his suicide.

As Mrs. Roberts, in retrospect, began to see a depressive pattern in her husband's behavior and symptoms, she heaped enormous guilt upon herself. "I should have known. . . . If only I'd insisted he see a doctor. . . . If only I'd gotten him to talk about it. . . . I shouldn't have been so engrossed in the children. . . . I should have paid more attention to him. . . ."

Firmly and carefully I explored Lois Roberts's guilt with her. I did not deny the bits of reality, I did not tell her not to feel guilty, I did not offer expiation. I explored.

"Wouldn't it have been wonderful if you *could have been* omniscient enough to predict his suicide? Wouldn't it have been wonderful if you could have been powerful enough to stop him? What happened when you did try to help him? Do you think with all the information we have now it is really possible to know why he committed suicide, why he chose the method he did, and the timing?" I asked many questions. Slowly she came to terms with the questions, the answers, and the lack of answers. Yes, there were symptoms of depression (sleeplessness, weight gain, argumentativeness), but they were sporadic and could be attributed to many causes. All of this put together would not have been sufficient to *force* him to get treatment; the only way his suicide could have been prevented was if *he* had wanted to prevent it. Sadly, she said, "I really did love him, but it wasn't enough. Loving and wishing don't make things happen any more than hating and wishing do . . . just as I tell Kevin."

It took eight months of individual and family sessions twice weekly before I felt the Roberts family was ready to be placed on follow-up. The weaning was gradual, first once a week, then every two weeks, then once a month, once every three months, then yearly. It has been eight years since Mr. Roberts's suicide. In the interim there were a number of difficult times during which the family returned for brief intervention. At three and a half Ned developed severe nightmares in which he saw "ghosts coming to get me." He was helped to understand the ghosts were his way of dealing with terrifying thoughts of his father returning to punish him for his supposed "badness," and he learned to talk and play out such thoughts. The nightmares disappeared quite quickly. When Kevin was eight he returned briefly after his dog had been poisoned. Furious, frightened, and utterly outraged, he needed to "talk about" what he was feeling. He healthily mourned his dog by talking about him and drawing many pictures of his pet from puppy to adulthood. Mrs.

Roberts returned two and a half years after her husband's death to talk about her concerns about remarriage. Essentially realistic and healthy, she had only residual bits of conflict—"It's really silly, but part of me feels disloyal to Curt. I don't want to do anything to hurt the boys"—which needed only minor intervention. On last follow-up the Roberts family was functioning well and happily.

My work with this family leaves several issues unanswered. Most painful of them, most frustrating for me is *why* Curt Roberts committed suicide. He said no good-byes, he left no explanatory note. Despite careful after-the-fact investigation of his psychology, behavior, and life stresses, the question remains unanswered. In designing the pattern of his last six months it became clear *upon investigation* that he was moderately depressed and therefore "at risk," but few of his symptoms could be construed as alarming, and certainly not by lay people. There was no history of sudden loss, suicide, or abandonment in his family at any anniversary date (when he was two-and-a-half or five; when his father had been his age; or when his parents had been married seven years, the length of his marriage, and so forth). He was creative and a perfectionist, but so are many people not at risk. Perhaps he had a "temporary aberration," as was suggested by many of his friends. I don't know. The "whys" of the timing of, reason for, and manner of his suicide remain a mystery. I am gratified his survivors remain healthy, and I shall attempt to insure their psychological health by continuing follow-up until Ned's second child is two-and-a-half, the last of many potential pathological anniversary dates.

There were no questions left unanswered when Enid Stern committed suicide. A research pharmacologist, she simply injected herself with enough morphine to kill ten people. Her death came as no surprise to her husband, Dan, her twenty-year-old daughter, Trish, her colleagues, her friends, or me. She had made sure of that—not by threatening or dropping clues, but by clear, well-reasoned, calm statements about her determination to end her life when it was no longer bearable.

Dr. Enid Stern had been dying of cancer; it had spread throughout her organs to her spine. No physician knew more about pain control than she did, and for several weeks before her death her pain had become increasingly intolerable. While still intellectually unimpaired, her body could no longer withstand the most minor exertion. Perhaps there was some special strength in Enid Stern that allowed her to share her thoughts and feelings with her family; certainly there was a special strength in Dan and Trish that allowed them to listen, hear, and respond with loving, sad understanding. Such strengths may have been born out of their capacity to bear helplessness in a situation over which no one had any realistic control, or perhaps it was born out of innate empathy and caring.

Dr. Stern had been open with her family throughout the eighteen months of her malignancy, to—and after—her death. She had shared her reasons and feelings for accepting or rejecting recommendations for treatment, letting her family know when she could cope and when she could not. She had also expressed her love for them *and* for herself. In a letter to her husband and daughter, she "absolved" them for responsibility or complicity in her death. She wrote, "You might be tempted to think I decided to kill myself to protect you from weeks or months of watching my agony. It would make me seem heroic, but would be true only in a tiny fraction. I do not want to watch your pain watching my pain. Most importantly, most selfishly, I do not have the temperament to be a martyr. I need to protect myself from what I know I cannot bear. . . . It is not my decision to abandon you, only the timing is mine. Despite this you will feel angry, resentful perhaps, even guilty, as I do. I am angry I have been cheated of my life, my work, my pleasures. . . . I am resentful of what I will have missed. . . . I feel guilt to have caused you pain. Above all I feel love for you both, and love for myself. And it is enough.''

It was almost enough. Dan and Trish Stern came to see me because they knew Enid and I had become close friends as well as ''therapeutic allies'' during her illness. They knew Enid had shared with me her decision to design her own death when her pain became unbearable and her life intolerable. Through painstaking discussion with Enid I had determined that her suicide plans were motivated by neither neurotic nor psychotic reasoning. She was not trying to escape life; she was trying to avoid agonized, dehumanized dying. She had elected not to include her family in her direct work with me. She believed she ''could handle'' preparing them for the course of her illness and her eventual death. As a rule I prefer to work with the entire family, but I agreed with Enid. She told me later that she had shared some of our work together with Trish and Dan (I usually recommend against ''diluting'' the alliance by discussing it with others, but again I agreed with Enid; it was helpful to all), and she requested them to see me together at least once after her death.

Unlike most suicidally bereaved families, neither Trish nor Dan Stern displayed any shame, horror, or surprise. Also unlike most bereaved families, they were singularly well prepared and supportive of her death by design. Trish was, however, still beset by ''There must have been something I could have done to make it easier,'' and Dan, also a physician, by ''I should have picked up the symptoms earlier, then maybe . . .''

I supported their wishes. ''It would have been a relief if there had been something else you could have done. It would have made you feel so much better if it had been possible to diagnose her illness earlier. It makes us feel so helpless when a disease remains silent until it's too late to cure it [for in fact Enid had not ignored or denied any symptoms—diagnosis came following a sudden hemorrhage]. The wishing is part of the guilt we feel merely by being alive and well, first when

Enid was sick, and now when she is dead. I feel it too."

The three of us shared our sadness and helplessness. We even expressed our anger, which we consciously displaced onto fate, viruses, and the limitations of modern technology to cure disease when it can send men to the moon. We grieved together, but it was apparent to me that they did not need me to help them mourn. I saw them again at Enid's funeral, and over the past several years I've gotten an occasional phone call, once when Enid's textbook was published posthumously, once when Trish got into graduate school to pursue a doctorate in biochemistry, once just to say "Hi—all's going well."

Several months after Enid's death I received a notebook. It came from Enid's lawyer and had my name on the cover. I knew Enid had kept a notebook for Trish and one for Dan; I didn't know she had kept one for me. It was really a diary, filled with observations, reflections, processes of decision making, and poems. On the first page was one sentence, "Ann, my dear, read this, and then use it in any way you will—maybe it could help someone else." I wept.

Perhaps it is the last poem she wrote before her suicide that can be the most helpful. It describes her awareness of turning inward to find her hidden self and her need to protect and comfort that self.

THE CHILD WHO IS ME

I hear you crying,
I cannot find you.
Hidden from me
Covered by me,
I have lost you.
Again.

Stuff of nightmare,
No road to follow,

Book to consult.
Only the thin thread
Of your screams
To guide me.

I lift the blanket.
You are not there.
Where are you?
It is very dark,
And I'm frightened too.
Keep crying, I am coming.
Then you shall cry no more.

Of all deaths, the most difficult to understand, and the most psychologically agonizing, is the suicide of a child. The death of a child from any cause makes a parent feel helpless. Functioning is impaired as one's sense of reliability and dependability plummet, and a child's suicide makes parents feel malignantly irresponsible and culpable. There is no disease, no reckless driver, piece of machinery, or natural disaster to blame. One's guilt precludes blaming the child, who is seen as "too young." The parents must blame themselves. I say "must," for the implacability of such parental guilt is awesome.

Jason Reynolds was fourteen when he took his father's gun and shot himself in the head. His suicide note read simply, "Dear Mom and Dad, I'm a born loser. I can't take it anymore. I'm sorry. You'll be better off without me. Love, Jason." The shot awoke nine-year-old Gerry in the next room. He ran into his brother's room to find him lying bloody and mutilated on the bed. Gerry's screams brought Howard and Joanne Reynolds racing in from the living room where they had been watching TV. Pushing Gerry and his mother out of the room and locking the door, Mr. Reynolds tried desperately to revive Jason. But he knew it was hopeless. The thirty-eight caliber gun had blown off the back of Jason's head. Dimly, through his shocked, disbelieving horror, Mr. Reynolds became aware of his younger son's shouting to his mother to wake up, and to his father for help. He covered Jason and went in the direction of the shouting to find his wife unconscious on the floor of their bedroom, with Gerry trying vainly to lift her into a sitting position. Without a word, Howard Reynolds lifted his wife onto the bed, brought a wet washcloth and put it on her forehead, then took Gerry by the hand and started for the front door. Gerry was crying and protesting and trying to pull away from his father. He kept crying that Jason and his mother were both dead. Mr. Reynolds held tightly to Gerry's hand and reassured him that his mother had just fainted and would be all right. He also told Gerry he was taking him to stay with the Fells, their next-door neighbors and good friends. Mr. Fell welcomed Gerry without any comment except that Gerry was always welcome. Mr. Reynolds left them. Within less than fifteen minutes Gerry had been abandoned by his brother, his mother, and finally his father.

I didn't see Gerry until the day after the funeral, and I saw him then only because he precipitated the referral.

Gerry had been kept at the neighbors throughout the three days between his brother's suicide and the funeral. His father visited him daily, but refused to allow him to return home because "everything is so chaotic" and "the Fells are taking very good care of you." The night his brother died, Gerry watched a stream of people entering and leaving his home. He saw Jason's body carried out on a stretcher, he saw the doctor arrive and the light go on in his parents' bedroom; he saw two policemen, the minister, his grandparents, his uncles, and some people he couldn't identify; but he did not see his mother. When his father visited him the following morning, Gerry begged to see his mother, but Mr. Reynolds refused, saying that his mother was too sedated but that he

could see her in a few days. Gerry asked about Jason, but his
father only kept repeating, "The gun must have gone off
while he was cleaning it." Gerry didn't believe him. He
knew Jason and Jason hated guns. He'd never spend a second
cleaning a gun. Gerry also knew his father. Mr. Reynolds
had taught his sons to respect guns, always to check to make
sure a gun wasn't loaded before cleaning, or even handling,
it. The gun case was always locked and there was only one
key, kept under his father's socks in his bureau. Jason would
have had to have stolen the key to get the gun. Most importantly, Gerry had seen the note. If his father had lied about
Jason, maybe he was lying about his mother, too. Gerry
made several attempts to sneak back into his own home, but
each time he was found by someone and returned to the
neighbors'—before he could see his mother. On the day of
the funeral Gerry dutifully left the Fells' house for school,
carrying his lunch bag and books. A block away he hid them
in the bushes and found a phone booth. He called the funeral
home he had overheard Mrs. Fell mention on the phone and
found out the time of the service. For the first time since his
brother's suicide, Gerry was given the information he was
seeking.

It was a very long walk. Gerry wanted to take his bike,
but there was no way to get it out of the garage without being
seen. He didn't dare hitch a ride; someone might ask him
why he wasn't in school. He arrived at the funeral home at
ten-thirty, a half hour before the service. He didn't know
what he was going to do—he just knew he had to see Jason
once more, and he had to see his mother.

At that moment a group of teenagers came in. Gerry
melted into the group and walked with them to see Jason. But
the casket was closed. What if there'd been a mistake, what if
it weren't Jason in there? Gerry stroked the smooth wood and
tried to remember how Jason had looked. He wondered if
Jason was still all bloody. He was very frightened. Then a

man came in and asked everyone to leave, announcing that the family wanted to be alone for a while. Gerry tried to hide himself among the kids, but suddenly he saw his parents as they saw him. His mother was walking in tiny steps, collapsed against his father. Her face was hidden behind a heavy veil. She screamed! And began to sob. His father's face tightened. "What are you doing here! You are supposed to be in school."

"Don't be mad, Dad, please. I had to say good-bye to Jase, Dad, I had to. Please, please, don't be mad." His mother reached out her arms and Gerry ran to her. Hugging and rocking, they sobbed together. It was the first time Gerry had been able to cry. Mr. Reynolds enfolded his wife and son in his arms, his face turned away so they could not see his tears.

Gerry didn't understand the funeral. Someone talked about "infinite wisdom," "mysterious ways," "the grief-stricken parents," "the bereft younger brother." No one talked about Jason. Now, with both parents crying, Gerry couldn't cry. He wondered what was the matter with him. He reached for his mother's hand, but she was holding herself as if she thought she would fall apart if she let go. He turned to his father, but before he could say a word he was told to be quiet and not upset his mother anymore. Gerry kept quiet.

Gerry remained quiet until his father brought him to see me the following day. On the phone Mr. Reynolds told me he was so worried about the way Gerry had "acted up" that he was following his minister's advice to "get help for Gerry." I told him I would like to see Gerry with both his parents. Mr. Reynolds refused. "My wife is much too upset, too heavily sedated. She doesn't have the strength to see you." I volunteered to come to the house. "This is a time when you all need one another very much. It is very important for your family to stay together. My job is not to further upset Mrs. Reynolds, it is to help her cope with what is already upsetting her so desperately.'' Howard Reynolds was adamant; he would come with Jason, but he would not bring his wife. I accepted his terms, hoping I would have a chance when we met to help him understand that his seemingly protective attitude was only making his wife less able to cope with Jason's suicide.

Within seconds of meeting me, Gerry began to talk. He told me everything I've reported to this point; the words poured out of him without a stop, even when his father interjected a statement of explanation. He told me how terrified he had been, how he was sure until he saw her that his mother was dead too. He said he couldn't get ''the sight of all the blood out of my head.''

I nodded. ''You can't get the sight of all the blood out of your head just like you couldn't make all the blood on Jason's head disappear. You have all kinds of frightening thoughts and questions about his death. You can't make yourself stop thinking about him. This is a good place to talk about all the ideas that are worrying and frightening you.''

He turned to his father. ''Dad, don't get mad, please. I know Jason wasn't cleaning the gun. I saw the note. Why did you lie to me? Why did he do it? Why, Dad? Tell me!''

Mr. Reynolds whispered, ''I didn't believe it. I thought you wouldn't know. I'm sorry, Gerry, maybe I shouldn't have lied to you. But I'm not lying now. I don't know why he did it. God help me! I'm his father and I don't know why my son killed himself. Why couldn't he have come to me? Why didn't I know how desperate he was? God forgive me, Joanne never will. And I'll never forgive myself!''

I didn't know whom to attend to first. I decided to attend to them together. ''It seems you're both expressing the same feelings in different ways. Gerry, twice in the last twenty minutes you've seemed afraid your dad would get mad at you. I wonder, does your dad get mad at you often—is that really what's making you afraid?''

They both looked at me in surprise and shook their heads.

"No," Gerry said, "Dad almost never gets mad at me. Sometimes he gets annoyed, but not really mad like Jase did."

"That's a very important thing to know. You have lots of thoughts of someone getting mad, but you know your dad rarely gets mad. Then you remember Jason got mad a lot. Maybe you got mad at him too. Maybe you feel as any brother would—you have an angry feeling toward Jason for killing himself, for doing it in such a horrifying way, even for deserting you. For most of us it's too frightening to think angrily about the dead, it's too scary to remember their anger; but all those angry thoughts have to go somewhere, and it's safe to think about your dad being angry because you're not really scared of *him*. Mr. Reynolds, you too have very angry feelings. But you turn your anger back on yourself. You blame yourself for 'not knowing,' for not having been able to prevent Jason's suicide. You are angrily punishing yourself as if you had the power to have known and stopped Jason. You say your wife won't ever forgive you either. That may or may not be true, but as long as she is isolated at home and so sedated that she cannot think clearly or share her grief, it will continue to remain inside her. The tranquilizers and sleeping pills cannot remove her pain; they can only delay it. As angry as you are with yourself, so she must be angry at herself; only you express it openly, she expresses it by withdrawing."

Mr. Reynolds nodded slowly. "You can't know what it's been like. She's been a zombie. I know she blames me, she'd have to. It was my gun, and she hated guns. But I never used them carelessly. And I only hunted for food, never just to kill. But my gun killed Jason. I was his father. It was my responsibility to protect him, not to set him up to commit suicide. Why didn't I know?"

"Mr. Reynolds, I know nothing about Jason except what I learned just now, that he was angry very often. For us even to begin to understand why he decided to kill himself, we are going to have to take a hard look at him. I will need to hear about him from all of you. We may or may not be able to understand his decision, you all may or may not have had a role in his decision, but I am sure of one thing—that you are all acting self-destructively, almost as if you were trying to get closer to Jason by being as self-hurtful as he was. I wonder if that's the only or the best way to mourn Jason. I think not. But to find other ways we must work together. You will need to remember all of Jason, not just his self-destruction. Mr. Reynolds, I would like to see you, your wife, and Gerry tomorrow. We have a great deal of hard work to do, and the sooner we begin the greater chance we have to do it well."

As they left the room Gerry turned back toward me and said, "I *am* mad at Jase. He shouldn't have done this, not to us, not to him. He shouldn't have done it!"

"Gerry, Jason must have been hurting very much to have hurt you and your parents so badly. But you have every right to be angry at him. That's something we can talk more about tomorrow. I'll see you then."

I saw the Reynoldses the next day, then twice a week for slightly more than a year, and came to learn a great deal about Jason, the family history, and the family "secrets." Jason was described by his parents and brother as a "wonderful kid . . . until a year ago." Mrs. Reynolds said he was a warm, friendly, mischievous boy who was, however, very sensitive. Mr. Reynolds agreed, adding "and he was wonderful with his hands, he could build anything, fix anything, and he was a really good tennis player." Gerry described his brother as having been "awfully bossy," but always ready to help him build models, help him with his homework, and even let him tag along with his friends. All agreed Jason was a perfectionist. Until a year ago. Then Jason changed. He became moody, was often withdrawn, flew off the handle "at nothing," and his grades dropped from honors to barely passing. His parents recalled that a lot was happening at the time. Jason was entering puberty, his body was changing rapidly, and he often complained his knees hurt, his legs ached, he "looked weird," and he "hated" how skinny and gangly he was. He began complaining that he was a "weirdo" and no one understood him. About the same time his maternal grandfather had a coronary attack and died. Jason had been quite close to his grandfather and seemed devastated by the loss. Several weeks later a close friend of Jason's was killed in a bike accident, then a tennis acquaintance had a leg amputated because of a lymphosarcoma.

Jason's withdrawal deepened. He avoided family meals and get-togethers; if he did join in he was provocative, irritable, and preoccupied with bodily complaints and the "uselessness of life." He would "spoil the fun" the family used to have with his "morbid preoccupation" with accidents, illness, skyjackings, kidnappings, pollution, street crime, and the "stupidity of the world." His parents tried to be patient, tried to talk with him, but he pushed them away. They thought it was just a "stage"; after all, "all adolescents have a rough time." From morbid concern about the stupidity of the world, Jason moved to constant criticism of his own inadequacies. He couldn't concentrate in school, he was "dumb." His coordination was "off," he played "lousy tennis." He was always tired, nothing interested him anymore. Increasingly concerned, his parents took him to his pediatrician who reported that Jason was slightly underweight, probably from poor eating habits like most teenagers, but was essentially healthy. "No cause for concern." They were also told that he was in an early but rapid growth spurt, and that he'd be fine when he hit his stride.

Both parents expressed how helpless they felt during

this time. Jason seemed unreachable. "Just leave me alone! . . . Don't bother about me!" became the sum of his communication. Gerry was often the butt of his anger. He constantly criticized Gerry for being lazy and irresponsible, a "pig"; and Gerry retaliated by calling Jason a "dumb weirdo." Again Mr. and Mrs. Reynolds sought help. They spoke to the guidance counselor at school, who agreed with their concern about Jason's school work but suggested that they were overanxious. The pediatrician also said he'd be glad to talk to Jason, but Jason refused to see him. They then consulted with a psychiatrist, who felt Jason's withdrawal and preoccupations with his "inadequacies" indicated a problem of greater severity than the expectable difficulties of adolescence, and recommended an evaluation for Jason. After much argument, Jason agreed to go, but managed to "forget" the appointment. Two days later he killed himself. No one at home, school, or among his friends knew of "anything special" that had occurred during those two days. No major crises, losses, or disappointments were discovered to give a clue to the timing of Jason's decision to kill himself. Long accustomed to his "morbid preoccupations," no one had noticed anything different in his communications or his behavior. His suicide was a shock to everyone.

Over the next few weeks, Mr. and Mrs. Reynolds were enmeshed in self-recriminations and angry accusations. They tried not to argue in front of Gerry, but a closed bedroom door was poor insulation for their pain and rage. Night after night Gerry overheard their shouts and sobs. They tried to be helpful by assuring him he was not responsible for his brother's problems or actions, but by then both had lost faith in their ability to parent, to protect, and to nurture their son. Their assurances sounded hollow to Gerry, who felt his world crumbling around him.

That the family continued to come regularly to their scheduled appointments was the only sign I saw for hope of their eventual return to healthy functioning. My work during this time revolved primarily around confronting them with how, in their grief and guilt, they were alienating themselves from one another in much the same way Jason had alienated himself from them. I acknowledged how hard they had tried to get help for Jason and pointed out that he had refused it. Now they were seeking help for themselves, but they were not allowing themselves or each other the closeness and sharing that would facilitate their healing. Each of their painful, angry actions and reactions was a reliving, an imitation, of the last year of Jason's life. It was as if they were saying, "Since I couldn't make Jason's life happy, I will never allow myself to be happy either."

It was several months before Mrs. Reynolds allowed herself to enter Jason's bedroom. She found a notebook and bottles of amphetamines and barbiturates secreted among his records and tapes. The pills were a shock. No one had suspected Jason of being on "uppers and downers," medication that, if taken indiscriminately, only serves to upset the body's biochemistry and increase both irritability and depression. But it was the notebook that truly exposed him—revealing as it did the vital clue to Jason's motive.

The handwritten journal had been begun nearly a year before Jason's suicide. It was filled with wrenching descriptions of how disappointed Jason felt about his body, his character, his achievements, and his acceptability to himself, his family, and the world. Each searing self-denigration was followed by "Jimmy never would have turned out like me," or "Jimmy would've had all his shit together," or "They lost the wrong one," or "I can't ever be what Jimmy was."

Who was Jimmy?!! Slowly, in whispers, their voices hollow with the echo of unresolved grief, Howard and Joanne Reynolds told me about Jimmy. I could feel their anguish. Jimmy had been their firstborn child. A handsome, sturdy, happy child, he filled his parents' expectations with joy. Then suddenly, at four and a half, Jimmy ran a high fever and thirty-six hours later he was dead. The Reynoldses were incapacitated with grief. How to explain to family and friends, "there was nothing anyone could do." How could life ever be worthwhile again? Protective friends, feeling Mrs. Reynolds would be "overwhelmed," urged her husband to keep her heavily sedated and away from Jimmy's funeral. Everyone had the same advice. "You're both still young. Time will heal. Have another baby as soon as possible." Sixteen months later they did. Jason was their replacement child, but Jason was never told about Jimmy. At least no one ever sat down and spoke to him directly about Jimmy. But Jason knew and lived with the secret burden of the "ghost" of his unknown brother. We will never know how many times the secret of Jimmy's existence leaked out in overheard words, in mixed messages, in subtle pressures; we do know Jason knew. His notebook was filled with the idealized Jimmy. And the unrealized Jason.

Ultimately there was no understanding the multiplicity of events, reactions, and fantasies that eventuated in Jason's decision to commit suicide. I do not believe that any one variable was *the* explanation. What we know is that all the variables somehow overloaded Jason to the point where he felt so helpless and hopeless that life had lost its value. As his parents were victimized by the death of their firstborn, so Jason was victimized by being unable to live up to the expectations he projected upon his parents; and by the competition with a long dead, never-to-be-matched, older sibling.

One question was left to be answered. Why did he choose the time that he did? What was its meaning? All of us who work with families in which there is a death by design look for anniversary reactions. The timing of a suicide is rarely incidental. It was the awareness of the power of such anniversary reactions, rather than brilliant intuition, that led me to ask the Reynoldses for the date on which Jimmy died. It was May 1. Jason killed himself on May 1.

None of these secrets emerged until four months after Jason's death. They helped explain the extraordinary resistance the Reynoldses had shown to mourning adaptively together. Unable to do the work of mourning for Jimmy, and thus to develop some immunization to the pathogenic aspects of future losses, they succumbed to the "guilt of the survivor." And like Jason, they were overloaded. Victimized by Jimmy's death, they received no adequate assistance in coping with their loss. Indeed they were encouraged to deny and avoid, rather than cope. Jason's suicide confirmed their most terrifying nightmare: they were incompetent, inadequate, destructive parents. No wonder they had abandoned Gerry psychologically; they felt they could only harm him too. It took many more months of work to sift through all the factors involved in their double bereavement. They needed to sort out factors beyond their control: Jimmy's untreatable illness and death, the death of Jason's grandfather and friend, Jason's developmental vulnerability as an adolescent, his pill-popping. They needed to recognize that they had made misjudgments in not sharing their "terrible secret." They needed to recognize that they were not omnipotent, that all their parental power was not sufficient to make Jason want to help himself. Once these needs were acknowledged, the agonizing work of mourning could begin under healthier, more adaptive, less punitive terms. As the sole surviving child, Gerry was at high risk. He needed to define himself as Gerry, not as a magical replacement for either Jason or Jimmy. And he needed his parents' support, to accept and love him for what he was—not for what his brothers were, or were thought to be.

Gerry is now fifteen. He has outlived the ages of Jimmy and Jason. In most areas he has mastered the dangers of being a survivor because he *knows* he is a survivor. He has the option of returning for help when things get rough, or when he feels frightened or depressed and can't quite figure out what's troubling him. He knows it is not his weakness that he is a survivor; it is his strength that he dares to deal with his status. Mr. and Mrs. Reynolds have done better than I would have predicted; they have learned to share their grief, guilt, and pain rather than use these feelings to punish themselves or each other. They are now able to invest their energy in helping Gerry grow increasingly strong. I don't believe they have resolved all their problems; I doubt they ever will. But they are functioning as a couple, as parents, and in their network of friends and work. And they are willing to bear the pain and enjoy the pleasure that go with being alive.

Many suicides cannot be prevented, but I am convinced it is possible to prevent the recurrence of suicide among those who survive, who feel themselves abandoned. Such prevention is not simply a matter of clinical intervention, but also of demanding better public education and social change. As long as our culture judges suicide as a sin or otherwise shameful, we will continue to impose the burdens of prolonged denial, avoidance, and maladaptive mourning practices upon the bereaved. Until our population is educated and sensitized to recognizing the vulnerabilities of those abandoned through suicide, we will continue to doom the survivors to repeat what has been inflicted on them. Again, it is not the sins of the fathers that are visited upon the children, it is the unresolved conflicts and guilts and fears of our families. We have a choice to identify with life or with death, with gratification or with loss, with productivity or stagnation, love or hate. We need courage to choose.

From
Victimization
to Mastery

8

Any external event that changes the balance of a person's life can be considered a situational crisis. Such events tend to disorganize and disrupt, to frustrate individual and family functioning and interactions. Such events make us all victims. Taking common and devastating life crises, I have tried in this book to define and reveal what victims experience; and to explore what kinds of intervention are adaptive or maladaptive. Since human psyches and defenses are in some ways similar from one individual to another, one type of crisis to another, I have had to repeat and stress certain points of adaptation: the healing value of sharing observable truths; the risks, on the other hand, of using truth as a club or a means of manipulation; the many guises of infantilization among victims and survivors, and of revictimization by well-meaning, if misguided, care-givers; the uses of psychological immunization; and, perhaps most persistently, the *hard work* of recovery and redirection.

In addition to having to cope with acute external events,

we are under daily pressures from within, from our own
consciences and sense of responsibility as parents, children, workers, and community members. Simultaneously
our society—so competitive, frantic, and instantly com-
municative—imposes pressure from without via our
jobs, our social interactions, our educational requirements,
our economics and politics. We are directed by such pressures to do, feel, and react in certain "acceptable" ways.
And when our feelings, actions, and reactions are not what
have been deemed acceptable, we feel guilty. Guilt can be
reactive, neurotic, or even existential, but it is certainly one
of our most common responses to pressure and stress. And in
times of crisis, it is usually what most interferes with adaptive functioning.

There are many sources of help for the victimized.
Community clinics and nonprofit agencies—where fees run
on a sliding scale from as little as fifty cents per session—are
available to facilitate constructive coping for stressed individuals and families. More and more self-help groups are
forming throughout the country, usually to help meet the
needs of people who have experienced a certain kind of victimization. There are groups for rape victims, battered wives,
single parents, families of alcoholics, mastectomy patients,
widows, bereaved parents. And in many communities there
are telephone hot lines to advise anonymous callers.

Increasingly, governmental agencies are applying themselves to the preventive and interventive needs of people.
There is now federal legislation mandating all states to provide primary medical prevention and early detection of physical and mental illness for children from birth to eighteen.
Yet as sensible and economical as the mandate is, I know of
no state that has systematically and conscientiously followed
it. Why? And why don't parents *demand* that the states follow it? Recently the National Center for the Prevention and
Control of Rape was founded under the joint aegis of the

Department of Health, Education, and Welfare, and the National Institute of Mental Health. The federal government sponsors psychological intervention for victims of natural disasters, but as yet none for victims of other types of disasters: hijackings, fires, explosions, and plane and train crashes. The government of Holland set an excellent example when the hostages held prisoner by the Moluccan terrorists in early June 1976 were taken immediately upon release for medical *and* psychological evaluation and intervention. Shouldn't we, with all our experience and expertise, provide the same for our citizens who survive public disasters?

Intervention on a local rather than a federal level is, of course, far more common. It may be governmentally or privately funded. A mental health clinic in Santa Clara, California, has capably and concernedly met the needs of victims of incest. Through a sensitive public and professional educational campaign, its staff has worked to break down the wall of resistance and shame isolating incestuous families in order to intervene therapeutically with the victims. In Marin County, California, a careful study is being made of the children of divorced parents, to track their growth, development, and problems. Several teaching hospitals in Massachusetts, Connecticut, and New York are conducting programs of model psychological intervention with dying patients and their families. A medical school in North Carolina and another in California are implementing programs to meet the special needs of foster children and foster parents. This list is far from complete, but it gives an idea of the growing public awareness of and attentiveness to the needs of victims.

One area of considerable progress has been in the recognition of stress as a potentially pathogenic experience. Knowledge and research that previously were disseminated only to professional groups in the same discipline are now beginning to be spread among all types of clinicians and to the general public. We have learned that stressed people suffer a higher-than-average incidence of accidents, depressive and anxiety reactions, and new infectious and malignant illnesses. We know that stress is one trigger for coronary disease, migraines, and ulcers. We have observed that stressed people pour out greater than normal amounts of corticoid hormones—hormones that operate to suppress the body's immunologic defenses (and are accordingly used to prevent rejection of donor organs and reduce inflammatory reactions) and thus make stressed people more susceptible to whatever bacterial, viral, or fungal pathogen is around them. Thanks to the open and ongoing work of the specialists—of biochemists, immunologists, endocrinologists, oncologists, and psychotherapists—we can now view stress-related illness in the proper context of an interrelated physical, psychological, and social process.

The Center for Preventive Psychiatry has been in existence for thirteen years, yet operators manning our telephone answering service still have trouble with the name. Time and again they greet the caller with a cheery "Good morning, the Center to Prevent Psychiatry." And we have to smile, not just at the malapropism but at how accurately if unwittingly it expresses the ultimate goal of the therapist, especially in the work of situational crisis intervention. In absolute terms this goal of dispensability will probably remain Utopian, but everyday we work toward it—trying our best to encourage and educate individuals and families to use *their own* resources. And in this effort we realize our continuing achievement. Human beings are enormously vulnerable, but they are also magnificently resilient and understanding. If victims only learn to acknowledge their vulnerability, they can seize the chance to exercise new options to grow strong and well. Having mastered an acute situational crisis, they emerge healthier than before, able to conduct their lives to full creative capacity.

Selected Bibliography

General Prevention and Intervention

Jackson, Edgar N. *Coping with the Crises in Your Life*. New York: Hawthorn, 1974. Clear exploration of origins of, preparation for, and resolution of life crises; humanistically and sensitively written by a minister and pastoral counselor.

Kliman, Gilbert. *Psychological Emergencies of Childhood*. New York: Grune & Stratton, 1968. Primarily a guide for educators, pediatricians, and psychiatrists; provides a rich source for sensitizing parents to children's vulnerabilities and strengths.

Lynch, James J. *The Broken Heart*. New York: Basic Books, 1977. "Simply put, there is a biological basis for our need to form and maintain human relationships. If we fail to fulfill that need, our health is in peril." A powerful argument for the relationship between loss, loneliness, and physical illness.

Ramos, Suzanne. *Teaching Your Child to Cope with Crises*. New York: McKay, 1975. Well written for parents and educators; emphasizes the early recognition of crises and structures the options for coping.

Death—Dying—Bereavement

Agee, James. *A Death in the Family*. New York: Bantam, 1971. A classic, fictionalized account of the effects of a death on a family.

Alsop, Stewart. *Stay of Execution*. Philadelphia: J.B. Lippincott, 1973. Diagnosis, treatment, pain, remissions—a famous journalist recounts his own feelings about his illness.

Becker, Ernest. *The Denial of Death*. New York: The Free Press, 1973. A cultural anthropologist's thesis that fear of death animates man.

Caine, Lynn. *Widow*. New York: Morrow, 1974. A moving personal account; what not to do and why.

Carr, Arthur C., ed. *Tolstoy's "Ivan Illych" A Commentary*, Bd. with *The Death of Ivan Illych*. New York: Health Science Publishing Corp., 1973. Powerful and poignant representation of a dying person's environment.

Fulton, Robert, and Bendiksen, Robert. *Death and Identity*. New York: John Wiley & Sons, 1965. Sociological orientation; collection of pertinent research of various aspects of death with extensive authors' commentary.

Furman, Erna. *A Child's Parent Dies: Studies in Childhood Bereavement*. New Haven: Yale University Press, 1974. Documentation of immediate reactions and long-term effects on a child's character and ability to pursue life.

Grollman, Earl A. *Talking About Death*. Boston: Beacon Press, 1974. Constructive, sensitive dialogue between parent and child.

Gunther, John. *Death Be Not Proud*. New York: Harper & Row, 1971. The raging, touching account of his son's dying and death.

Hendin, David. *Death as a Fact of Life*. New York: W.W. Norton, 1973. Medical journalist surveys issues on death and dying.

Jackson, Edgar N. *Telling a Child About Death*. New York: Hawthorn, 1965. Plea for honesty; nature of children's reactions at various ages.

Kastenbaum, Robert, and Aisenberg, Ruth. *The Psychology of Death*. New York: Springer, 1972. Psychological aspects of death, accident, illness, murder, and suicide; text and references.

Kubler-Ross, Elizabeth. *Questions and Answers on Death and Dying*. New York: Macmillan, 1974. Exploration and documentation of the stages of dying.

Kutscher, Austin H., ed. *Death and Bereavement*. Springfield, Ill.: Charles C. Thomas, 1974. Nineteen eclectic contributions divided into "Dying and Death," "Philosophy—Religion—Survival," "Bereavement," "Practicalities of Recovery from Bereavement," "Care of the Bereaved," "Rebirth of the Spirit," and an annotated bibliography.

LeShan, Eda. *Learning to Say Good-by: When a Parent Dies*. New York: Macmillan, 1977. A powerful and poignant account of bereaved children, their feelings, and adult reactions; plea for sharing truths.

Mills, Gretchen C., et al. *Discussing Death: A Guide to Death Education*. Homewood, Ill.: E.T.C. Publications, 1975. Implementation guide for educating children from preschool through college.

Parkes, Colin M. *Bereavement: Studies of Grief in Adult Life*. New York: International Universities Press, 1972. Case-study approach; well-written compilation of research findings.

Shepard, Martin. *Someone You Love Is Dying: A Guide for Helping and Coping*. New York: Crown, 1975. Lay discussion of major terminal illnesses; practical information on insurance, wills, and so forth.

Stein, Sara Bonnett. *About Dying* (Open Family Series). New York: Walker, 1974. Written with the consultation and enthusiastic approval of the Center for Preventive Psychiatry, a book with documentary photographs meant to be read by young children and parents together.

Wolitzer, Hilma, *Ending*. New York: Morrow, 1974. A young husband and wife wait together for his death; brave and beautiful.

Handicaps

Alexanian, Alexander. *An Investigation into Public and Private Attitudes Held Toward Various Handicapped Groups, Stutterers, Cerebral Palsied, and the Blind*. San Francisco: R&E Research Associates, 1975.

Belgum, David. *What Can I Do About the Part of Me I Don't Like?* Minneapolis: Augsburg, 1974.

Ellingson, Careth, and Cass, James. *Directory of Facilities for the Learning-Disabled and Handicapped*. New York: Harper & Row, 1972.

Galbreaith, Patricia. *Hints for the Handicapped*. New York: Drake, 1974.

Gutman, Ernest M. *Travel Guide for the Disabled*. Springfield, Ill.: Charles C. Thomas, 1967.

Haskins, James. *A New Kind of Joy: The Story of the Special Olympics*. New York: Doubleday, 1976.

Lancaster-Gaye, Derek, ed. *Personal Relationships, the Handicapped and the Community: Some European Thoughts and Solutions*. Boston: Routledge & Kegan Paul, 1972.

Myers, J. S. *Orientation to Chronic Disease and Disability*. New York: Macmillan, 1965.

Sobol, Harriet L. *My Brother Steven Is Retarded*. New York: Macmillan, 1977. Sensitive text and photography; how a "normal" sister feels about her mentally retarded brother.

Stein, Sara Bonnett. *About Handicaps* (Open Family Series). New York: Walker, 1974. See comments on series under "Death—Dying—Bereavement."

Hospitalization

Blesky, Marvin S., and Gross, Leonard. *How to Choose and Use Your Doctor*. New York: Fawcett World Library, 1976.

Bergmann, Thesi, and Freud, Anna. *Children in the Hospital*. New York: International Universities Press, 1966. Brilliant and aware description of children's reactions to illness and the relationship between children's characters and their recovery rate.

Dickens, Doris. *You and Your Doctor*. Hicksville, N.Y.: Exposition Press, 1973.

Field, Minna. *Patients Are People*. New York: Columbia University Press, 1967. Emphasis on the practice of treating people rather than causes.

Gaver, Jessyca R. *How to Help Your Doctor Help You*. New York: Pinnacle Books, 1975. The author guides patients to know their rights and to exercise them with the physician as ally.

Ramsey, Paul. *The Patient As Person: Exploration in Medical Ethics*. New Haven: Yale University Press, 1970. For physicians, all hospital staff, *and* patients.

Stein, Sara Bonnett. *A Hospital Story* (Open Family Series). New York: Walker, 1974. See comments on series under "Death—Dying—Bereavement."

Travis, Georgia. *Chronic Illness in Children: Its Impact on the Child and the Family*. Stanford: Stanford University Press, 1976.

Separation and Divorce

Athearn, Louise M. *What Every Formerly Married Woman Should Know*. New York: McKay, 1973. Psychological, legal, and social self-defense for divorced women.

Atkin, Edith, and Rubin, Estelle. *Part-Time Father*. New York: Vanguard, 1976. Problems, priorities, and possibilities for fathers with rights of visitation.

Despert, J. Louis. *Children of Divorce*. New York: Doubleday, 1970.

Fisher, Esther O. *Divorce: The New Freedom*. New York: Harper & Row, 1974. Divorce explored as a new opportunity.

Gardner, Richard. *Boys and Girls Book About Divorce*. New York: Aronson, 1971. For children, written clearly and honestly by a child psychiatrist highly experienced in working with children of divorce.

Gilder, George. *Naked Nomads: Unmarried Men in America*. New York: Quadrangle, 1974. Explores the problems that beset divorced men.

Kessler, Sheila. *The American Way of Divorce: Prescriptions for Change*. Chicago: Nelson-Hall, 1975. The title admirably describes the long overdue material well covered in this book.

McKenney, Mary. *Divorce: A Selected Annotated Bibliography*. Metuchen, N.J.: Scarecrow Books, 1974.

Sherwin, Robert V. *Compatible Divorce*. New York: Universal Publishing and Distributing, 1970.

Vollmer, Howard M. *Going Through Divorce: Facing the Problems of Adjustment*. Palo Alto: Pacific Books, 1975.

Wheeler, Michael. *No-Fault Divorce*. Boston: Beacon Press, 1974. A civilized, sensible approach.

Rape—Sexual Molestation—Incest

Amir, Menachem. *Patterns in Forcible Rape*. Chicago: University of Chicago Press, 1971.

Astor, Gerald. *A Question of Rape*. Chicago: Playboy Press, 1975.

Brownmiller, Susan. *Against Our Will*. New York: Simon & Schuster, 1975. Brilliant exploration and analysis of all aspects of rape—historical, political, sociological, and psychological.

Hilberman, Elaine. *The Rape Victim*. New York: Basic Books, 1976. Primarily for professionals, this book nevertheless provides a balanced picture of the rape victim and her environment.

Macdonald, John M. *Rape: Offenders and Their Victims*. Springfield, Ill.: Charles C. Thomas, 1975.

Schultz, LeRoy G. *Rape Victimology*. Springfield, Ill.: Charles C. Thomas, 1975.

Suicide

Alvarez, A. *The Savage God: A Study of Suicide*. New York: Random House, 1972. Emphasis on the creative process and suicide.

Beck, Aaron T., et al. *The Prediction of Suicide*. Bowie, Md.: Charles Press, 1974. A thoughtful approach to a complex and disputed problem.

Cain, Albert C., ed. *Survivors of Suicide*. Springfield, Ill.: Charles C. Thomas, 1972. Survivors being defined as the family, both nuclear and extended, of successful suicides; a clinical and compassionate assessment of family vulnerabilities.

Grollman, Earl A. *Suicide*. Boston: Beacon Press, 1971. Warm, knowledgeable, and respectful of our humanness; a clergyman deals honestly with suicide and its ramifications.

Klagsbrun, Francine. *Too Young to Die: Youth and Suicide*. Boston: Houghton Mifflin, 1976. Straightforward information about youthful suicide; sensitively written, it explores the myths and realities of conditions leading to suicide, the anguish of families, and changing attitudes.

Lester, David. *Why People Kill Themselves: A Summary of Research*

Findings on Suicidal Behavior. Springfield, Ill.: Charles C. Thomas, 1972.

Shneidman, Edwin S., and Farberow, Norman L. *Clues to Suicide*. New York: McGraw-Hill, 1957. Two highly respected thanatologists describe the danger signals people can recognize.

Tabachnick, Norman, et al. *Accident or Suicide: Destruction by Automobile*. Springfield, Ill.: Charles C. Thomas, 1973. A careful inquiry into the confusion between accidents and suicides.

Wolman, B. B., and Krauss, H. H., eds. *Between Survival and Suicide*. New York: Halsted Press, 1975.

Epilog

Since I wrote this book we have learned a great deal, changed our frontiers, explored new concepts, and examined old skeletons long hidden in our collective closets. I am pleased that so much of what the book contains is still valid. I am gratified that the work of The Center for Preventive Psychiatry with bereaved children and their families continues to be replicated in such diverse settings as the "Good Grief" program at Boston's Judge Baker Clinic and Israel's community mental health clinics. I am reassured to see clinics and agencies emerging to better meet the needs of crime victims, abused spouses, disaster victims, families living with chronic and acute illness, and the like. But two chapters of this book need to be expanded: We can no longer ignore the issues of sexual abuse of children and youthful suicide.

Current statistics are simple and astonishing. One of every four females, and one of every ten males, reports childhood sexual abuse. Sexual abuse does not necessarily mean rape, but it is abuse nevertheless. Ignorance and embarrassment on the part of both family and community have colluded in the damage done to children. Myths we have retained interfere with appropriate protection of children and isolation of pedophiles. Sexual abusers of children do not self-correct. Before being apprehended, the average child molester abuses more than sixty children. Pedophiles may be male or female, heterosexual or homosexual or bisexual. Pedophilia is democratic; it is represented in every racial, religious, social, educational, and geographical group. Pedophiles may be members of the nuclear or extended family, friends of the family, or complete strangers. They may seduce or rape children. Such individuals use psychological and physical force as well as intimidation to ensure secrecy. Fewer than one in every two hundred children lie when they report sexual abuse.

Sexual abuse of childen not only indicates the pathology of the pedophile and the victimization of the child, but also clearly demonstrates the collusion of our society. As a child advocate, a parent, and a psychotherapist, I have become very angry. I intend to make my readers angry too. I also intend to use our anger productively and not waste its energy on palliatives or displaced vendettas. Aggressive energy fuels learning, and with enough energy we can learn to protect our children appropriately.

Several cases of child sexual abuse have come to national attention recently. In more than one of them, dozens of children were involved. Children had been infected with one or more venereal diseases, which went misdiagnosed and untreated for months. Children developed sleep and eating disorders, major school problems — both academic and social — and major regressive and aggressive symptoms. Many became provocative or withdrawn. Initially no one responded appropriately, because no one wanted to believe such abuse was possible. Few were willing to ask the right questions or listen to the children's statements. Everyone made self-protective assumptions. Pediatricians assumed poor hygiene; teachers assumed attention deficit disorders; parents assumed it was "just a phase"; neighbors assumed inadequate discipline. In several cases, even after incontrovertible proof of sexual abuse was discovered, parents, schools, and the community at large did not want to believe that such abuse had occurred. The few who had the courage to investigate (child protective services, the police, and child psychotherapists) were vilified for "making trouble" or "drumming up business."

It is not difficult to understand why adults in general, and parents in particular, are unwilling to confront the issue of sexual abuse of children. Confrontation destroys the illusion of childhood innocence; it means discussing sexual and aggressive issues with the children; it arouses guilt and a sense of failure in parents; it subjects the children to the strain of a legal investigation and potential grand jury and jury trial. Perhaps most anxiety provoking, it makes the family's private life very public indeed. But if we are to act responsibly, none of this should be enough to stop us from helping our children recover from the trauma of sexual abuse.

It is less disturbing and more effective to educate our children to prevent sexual abuse. Even preschoolers can be taught that it is not only safe, but necessary, to tell Mommy or Daddy about secrets that others want kept. Even very young children can learn that there is a difference between a "good touch" and a "bad touch." Children can be taught that they have a right to say no to anyone who wants them to do something that feels "scary" or strange or too exciting. Children old enough to walk alone to school or the store can be taught to yell at anyone who attempts to grab or molest or entice them, "You're not my mother [father]! Don't you touch me!" or even "Fire!" (people always respond to that). Neighborhoods can organize into community watches and publicize "safe houses," homes or stores that display large stickers on the doors or windows proclaiming them to be safe places for children to run to when they are endangered.

When prevention has been ineffective or impossible, immediate therapeutic intervention is obligatory. It is crucial that parents help their children understand that the rape or seduction was not the child's fault but, rather, the fault and responsibility of the perpetrator. Children must be helped to understand that they were victims, no matter what they were told, no matter what they felt. The entire community should act as a support system for the sexually abused child and family, rather than treat them as contaminated.

It has been my experience that it assists healing when children can cooperate in the judicial process of apprehending and prosecuting the child abuser. Identifying the perpetrator and testifying in court move the child from being a helpless, passive victim to being an active, coping survivor. What is not helpful is the practice of having many people (some of whom know little about child development or vulnerability) interview and interrogate the child. Those in our law enforcement and legal systems must be made more aware of the potential for revictimizing children at the very time they believe they are protecting them.

Family therapy is always mandated when the child abuse is incestuous. Abuse cannot occur within a family without severe pathology being shared, actively or passively, among family members. To enable the child to heal, and to learn to trust again, the family's sickness must be acknowledged and treated before the family members, individually and collectively, can be trusted. The stress I place on immediate and intensive psychotherapeutic help for sexually abused children and their families is pragmatically based. Sexually abused children grow up to abuse their own children sexually unless they are helped to break the chain. Perhaps it is a repetition compulsion. Perhaps it is an unconscious identification with the aggressor. Whatever the combination of dynamics, this aspect of sexual abuse of children is preventable.

Childhood and adolescent suicide has reached epidemic proportions in the United States over the past decade. A youthful suicide is attempted every forty seconds. Again, ignorance and embarrassment have frustrated adequate prevention, interventions, and postvention. The myths about youthful suicide blind and paralyze us and increase the emotional isolation felt by our desperate and depressed children. The most commonly held myths include: Those who talk about suicide don't do it; suicide threats or attempts are merely a bid for attention or a manipulation; suicidal ideas in kids will go away if you ignore them; someone who has attempted suicide and failed will not try again; suicide is an act of courage; if you talk to youngsters about suicide, you will put ideas in their heads; suicide can never be prevented; girls talk about suicide, but boys do it. All these myths are untrue. They lead us — and, more important, our children — into a dangerous sense of false security.

Like sexual abuse of children, suicide is often a vertical epidemic, flowing destructively from one generation to the next. It may also skip one generation and recur several times in the following one. Suicide often reflects an unconscious identification with a relative who committed suicide before. It also may reflect the individual's long history of loss and deprivation. There is a ripple effect from the experience of older family members who are still suffering from unresolved conflicts and uncompleted mourning and may lack sufficient energy to invest in the current generation. Even when the previous death of a parent, child, or sibling has not been a suicide, the adults' depressive reactions and emotional withdrawal from children put children at high risk for suicide.

As it frequently takes an entire family system to collude in producing suicidal ideas in the minds of young people, it also takes the entire family, nuclear and extended, to prevent that suicide. Indeed, the more angry and helpless families feel when confronted by a child's attempted suicide, the more urgently network intervention is needed. Network intervention involves assembling all the people who are significant in the lives of the distressed family. As friends and relatives gather around a physically ill person to lend support and demonstrate love, so must they gather around the person in severe psychological pain. They must offer support and love at the very time the individual is feeling that "there is not enough to live with, there is not enough to live for." Thus, the therapeutic task is to help the entire family system before it is too late.

Jodie Kliman, Ph.D., one of my staunchest supporters and most honest critics, recently gave me the quotation in the last paragraph while we were discussing Chapter 7 of this book. We agree that Lois Roberts should have gone for therapeutic help herself when her husband, Curt, first started showing depressive signs. The therapist could have helped her to help him enter family therapy, even if he refused to get help for himself alone. The gathering together of the entire family would have demonstrated to Mr. Roberts that everyone cared (enough to live with), and that everyone loved and valued him (enough to live for). The same applies to the Reynolds family. Jason's depressive symptoms appeared a year before his suicide. Family therapy was critically needed at that time. Certainly his grandfather's death should have mandated intervention for a family that not only was currently bereaved, but also had a history of incompleted mourning for its firstborn son. Primary prevention and common sense would have mandated that Mr. and Mrs. Reynolds enter therapy fifteen years before, immediately following the sudden death of their son Jimmy. Perhaps if adequate mourning had been facilitated at that time, the Reynolds could have released the energy that remained tied up in Jimmy's death and invested it in each other and in their younger children.

This postscript is not written to assign blame to the Roberts or Reynolds families, or to the families of anyone who commits suicide. It is intended to educate, alert, and even pressure families into giving up their ignorance and denial about youthful suicide. I know of no pain equal to that experienced by the parents of a child who commits suicide. Their loss is not only the loss of a child—it is also the loss of the hopes and dreams invested in that child. It is a loss of a piece of oneself, of self-esteem, of self-respect. It is a loss of the belief that one is a protective and adequate parent. It is a loss not only of the past, but of the future.

The concept of anniversary reactions warrants repeated emphasis. Anniversary reactions are usually, but not always, unconscious. They are reflected in multiple ways: actual anniversary, birthday, day of death, and holiday dates. They also include more hidden anniversaries, such as being the same age as the dead person, having a child the same age as the dead person had at the time of death, and reaching the same level of accomplishment (or failure) as did the dead person. If we remain aware of anniversary reactions, we will be able to reexperience the pain and distress consciously and non-judgmentally—and thus constructively rather than destructively.

Parents do not carry the sole responsibility for preventing childhood and adolescent suicide. Such prevention is also the responsibility of social agencies, physicians, mental health workers, clergy, and educators. Schools have an extraordinary opportunity to implement programs in suicide prevention, intervention, and postvention. Over the past seven years I have developed a pragmatic outline that I use in consultation with schools, nursery school through high school. I am never pleased when asked to consult with school personnel following a student's suicide. I am less displeased when asked to consult following a student's aborted suicide attempt. I am delighted when asked to consult with a school system solely because they are interested in preventing student suicide and are invested in educating and sensitizing all school personnel.

The following outline is generally presented in three consecutive 90-minute workshops. It has, when necessary, been condensed into a single two-hour presentation. It requires a minimum of a full day to explore in depth.

Childhood and Adolescent Suicide Prevention,
Intervention, and Postvention Workshops for Schools

I. A Look at Suicide Today: Suicide Prevention
   A. Myths
   B. Variables at Different Age Levels
   C. Depression
      1. Reactive
      2. Neurotic
      3. Psychotic
   D. The Romanticization and Libidinization of Death
   E. Responsibility
      1. The schools
      2. The parents
      3. The peers
      4. The community
   F. Epidemiology and Contagion
   G. Opportunities for Prevention
II. Intervention
   A. Early Recognition
   B. Evaluating the Risk
   C. Establishing a System of Referral and Support
   D. The Trap of Confidentiality: Confidentiality never
      applies when a life is at stake
   E. The Traps of Avoidance and Denial
   F. Establishing an Alliance with Parents
   G. Establishing an Alliance with the Psychother-
      apeutic, Medical, and Pastoral Community
   H. Educating School Personnel, Parents, and
      Students
   I. The Importance of Follow-up
III. Postvention: The School's Response
   A. Immediate Meeting of All School Personnel with
      an Experienced Therapist
      1. To share information and prevent distortion
      2. To provide a support system for all personnel

3. To prepare all personnel to meet the needs of the students
   a. Out-of-phaseness of school personnel
   b. Out-of-phaseness of students
   c. Out-of-phaseness of parents
   d. To assess the urgency of those at risk, especially family members, closest friends, etc.
4. To organize and establish
   a. Special events at school
   b. Guidelines for assisting students
      1. To express grief, anger, resentment, guilt, depression
      2. To talk to experienced therapists when necessary or desirable
      3. To deglorify the suicide: It is not heroic
      4. To communicate with each other and their families.

B. After-School Meeting for All Personnel

C. Follow-up

D. Follow-up One Year Later: Preparation for Anniversary Reactions

The usefulness of this outline is not limited to schools. I wish that the information it contains would become as familiar to everyone as the precaution of looking both ways before crossing a street. It is my hope that this revised edition of *Crisis* will facilitate that awareness.

Ann S. Kliman

Bibliography

Sexual Abuse of Children

Adams, Caren, and Fay, Jennifer. *No More Secrets: Protecting Your Child from Sexual Assault.* San Luis Obispo, Calif.: Impact Publishers, 1981.

Armstrong, Louise. *Kiss Daddy Goodnight: A Speak-Out on*

Incest. New York: Hawthorne Books, 1978. Pocket
    Book, 1979.
Burgess, Ann; Groth, A. Nicholas; Holmstrom, Linda L.;
    and Sgroe, Suzanne M. *Sexual Assault of Children and
    Adolescents.* Lexington Mass.: Lexington Books, 1978.
Finkelhor, David. *Sexually Victimized Children.* New York:
    The Free Press, Macmillan Publishing Company, 1979.
——. *Child Sexual Abuse: New Theory and Research.* New
    York: The Free Press, 1984.
Forward, Susan, and Craig, Buck. *Betrayal of Innocence:
    Incest and Its Devastation.* New York: Penguin Books,
    1979.
National Center on Child Abuse and Neglect. *Sexual Abuse
    of Children: Selected Readings.* Seattle, Wash.: Region X
    Child Abuse and Neglect Center, 1980.
Olson, Marlys. *Child Sexual Abuse: A Collaborative Ap-
    proach to Prevention and Treatment.* Tacoma School
    District Administration Building. Tacoma, Washington.
Sanford, Linda T. *The Silent Children: A Book for Parents
    about Prevention of Child Sexual Abuse.* Garden City,
    N.Y.: Anchor Press/Doubleday, 1980.
Schultz, Leroy G. *The Sexual Victimology of Youth.* Spring-
    field, Ill.: Charles C. Thomas, 1980.
U.S. Department of Health and Human Services. *Child Sexual
    Abuse: Preventive Tips to Parents.* Government Printing
    Office, 1984. 0-454-460: QL 3
Yates, Alayne. *The Eroticized Child.* Unpublished paper
    presented at the First World Congress of Victimology.
    Washington, D.C., August 1980.

Childhood and Adolescent Suicide

Griffin, Mary, and Felsenthal, Carol. *A Cry For Help.* New
    York: Doubleday, 1983.
Plotkin, D. *Children's Anniversary Reactions Following the
    Death of a Family Member.* Canada's Mental Health,
    June 13–15, 1983.

Raphael, B. *The Anatomy of Bereavement*. New York: Basic Books, 1983.

Rueveni, Uri. *Networking Families in Crisis*. New York: Human Science Press, 1979.

Rueveni, Uri; Speck, Ross; and Speck, Joan. *Therapeutic Intervention: Healing Strategies for Human Systems*. New York: Human Sciences Press, 1982.

Shneidman, Edwin. *Definition of Suicide*. New York: John Wiley & Sons, 1985.

Trimble, David; Kliman, Jodie; Villapiano, Albert; and Beckett, William. Follow-up of a full-scale network assembly. *International Journal of Family Therapy*. 6 (2): 102–113, 1984.

Death

Krementz, Jill. *How It Feels When a Parent Dies*. New York: Alfred A. Knopf, 1983.

Divorce

Krementz, Jill. *How It Feels When Parents Divorce*. New York: Alfred A. Knopf, 1984.